Women

of all ages

Kerwin FLEURIAL

The set of drawings you will find in this collection is a rendering of women of all ages and walks of life, a candid and intriguing view of what one's daughter, mother or grandmother might look like. The young girls, the charming women, the elegant and more mature ladies that are depicted in this one of a kind coloring book are who you want them to be. One of those authentic ladies might actually be you. While they are an original product of the artist's imagination, now that they are in your hands they are yours to transform and embellish. Please enjoy adding colors to their lives, and therefore yours.

CONTENTS

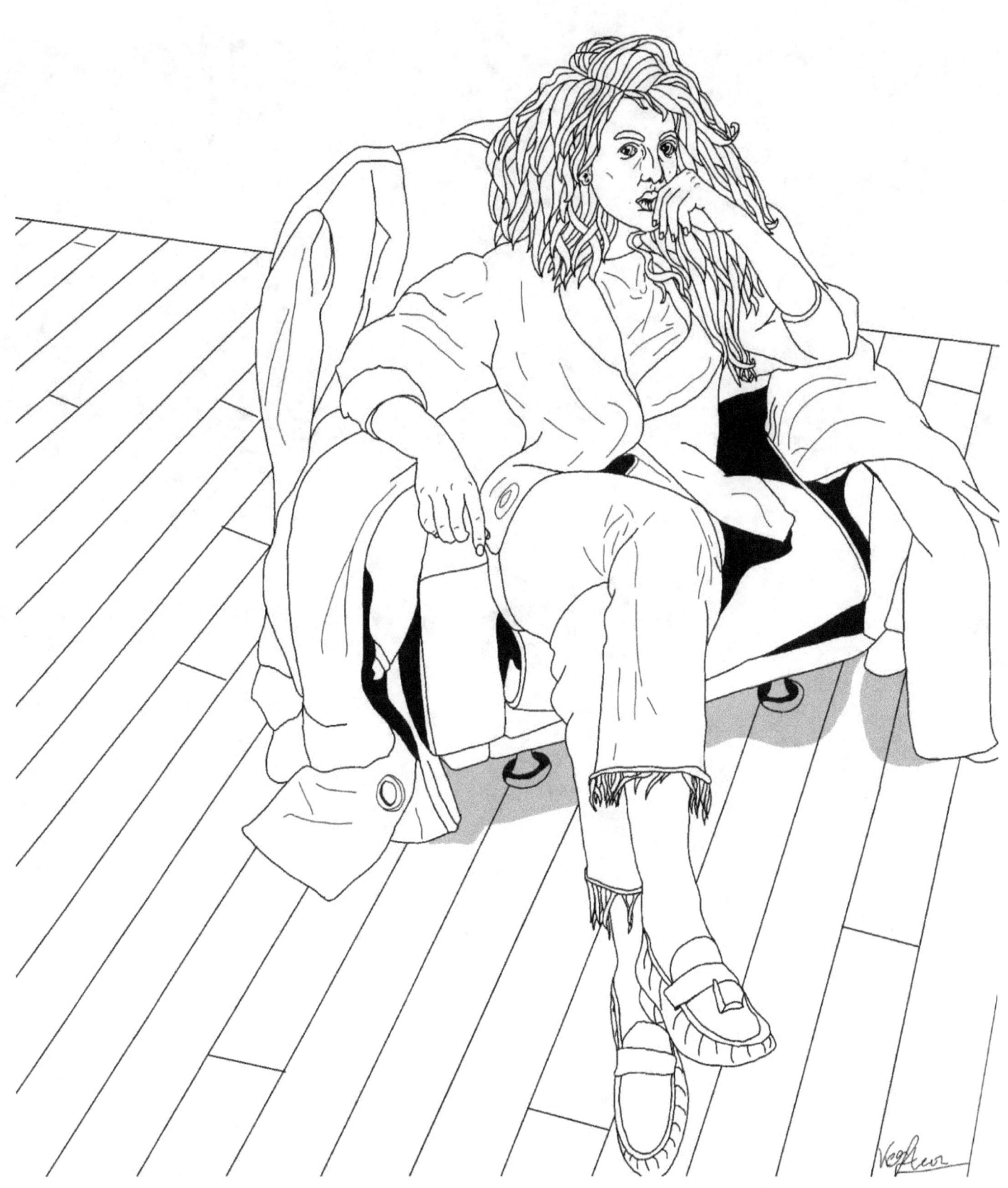

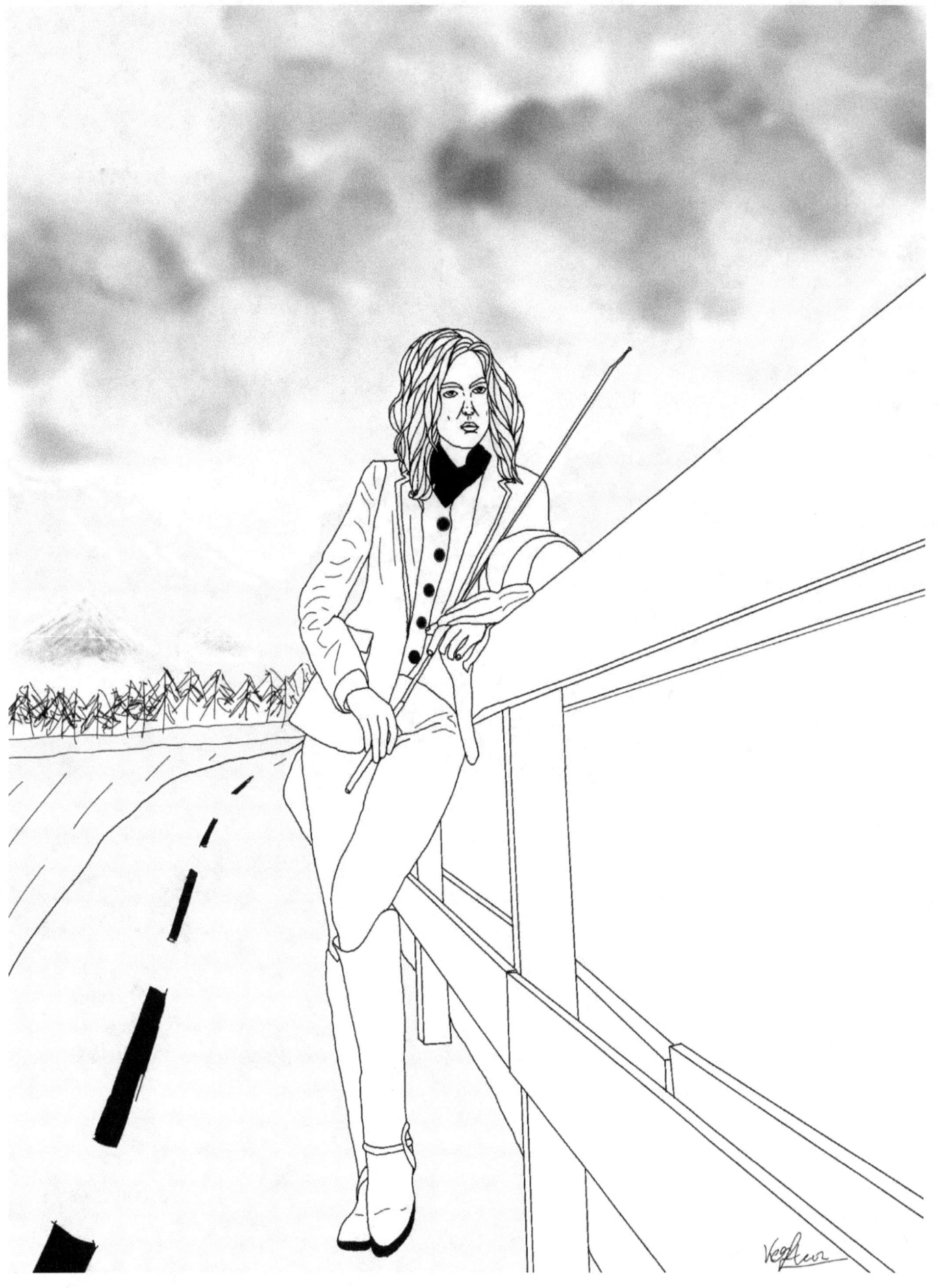

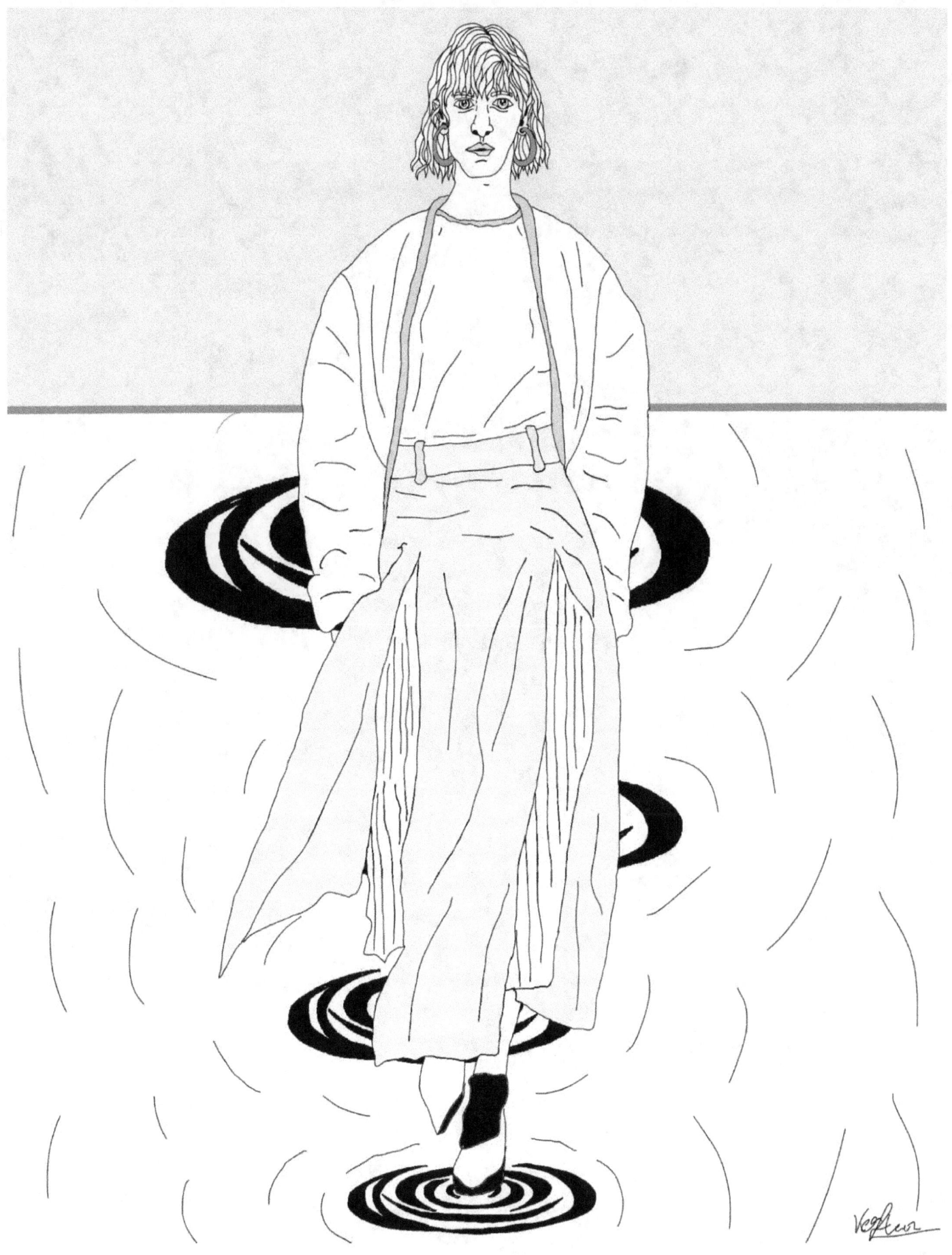

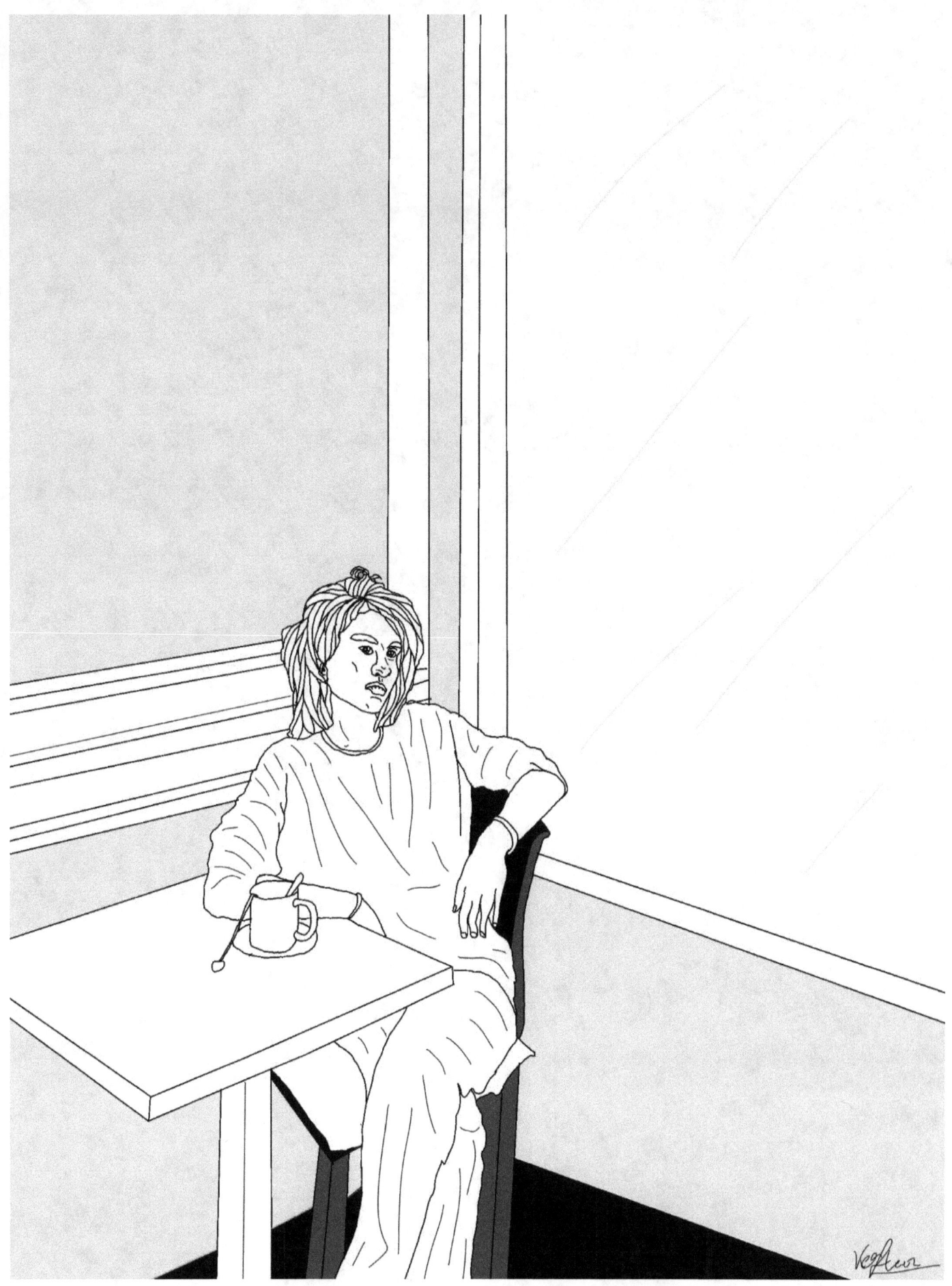

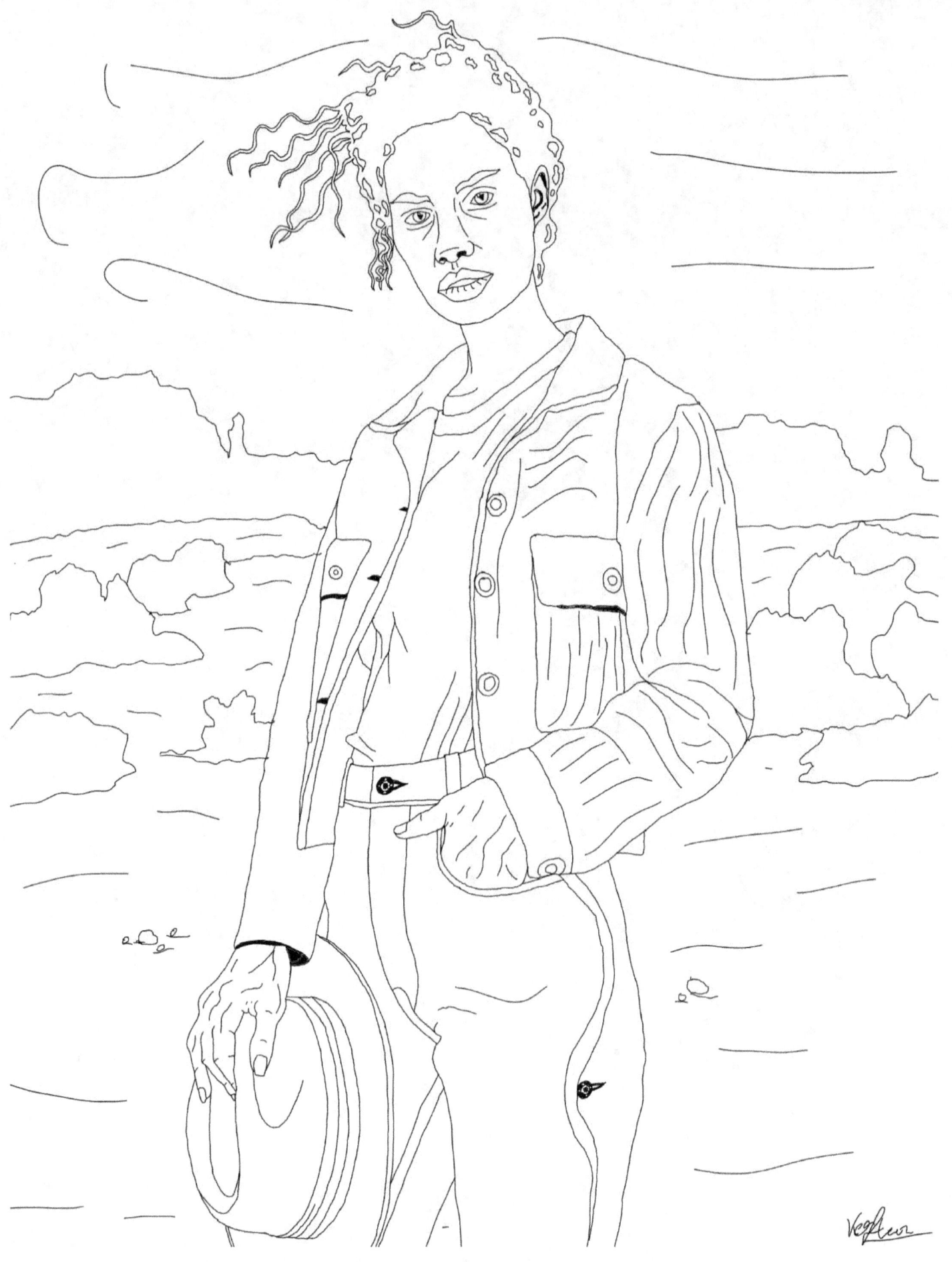

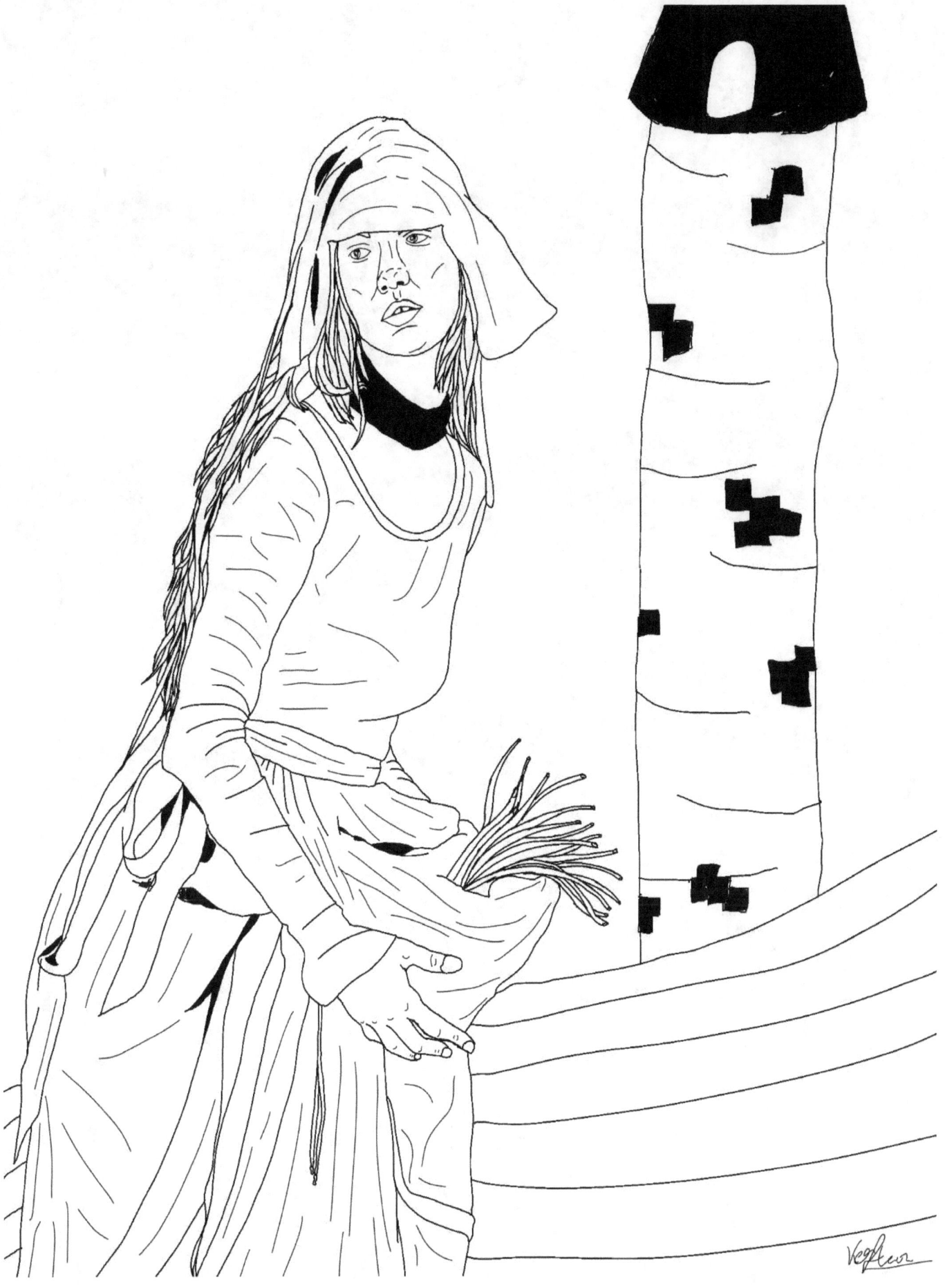

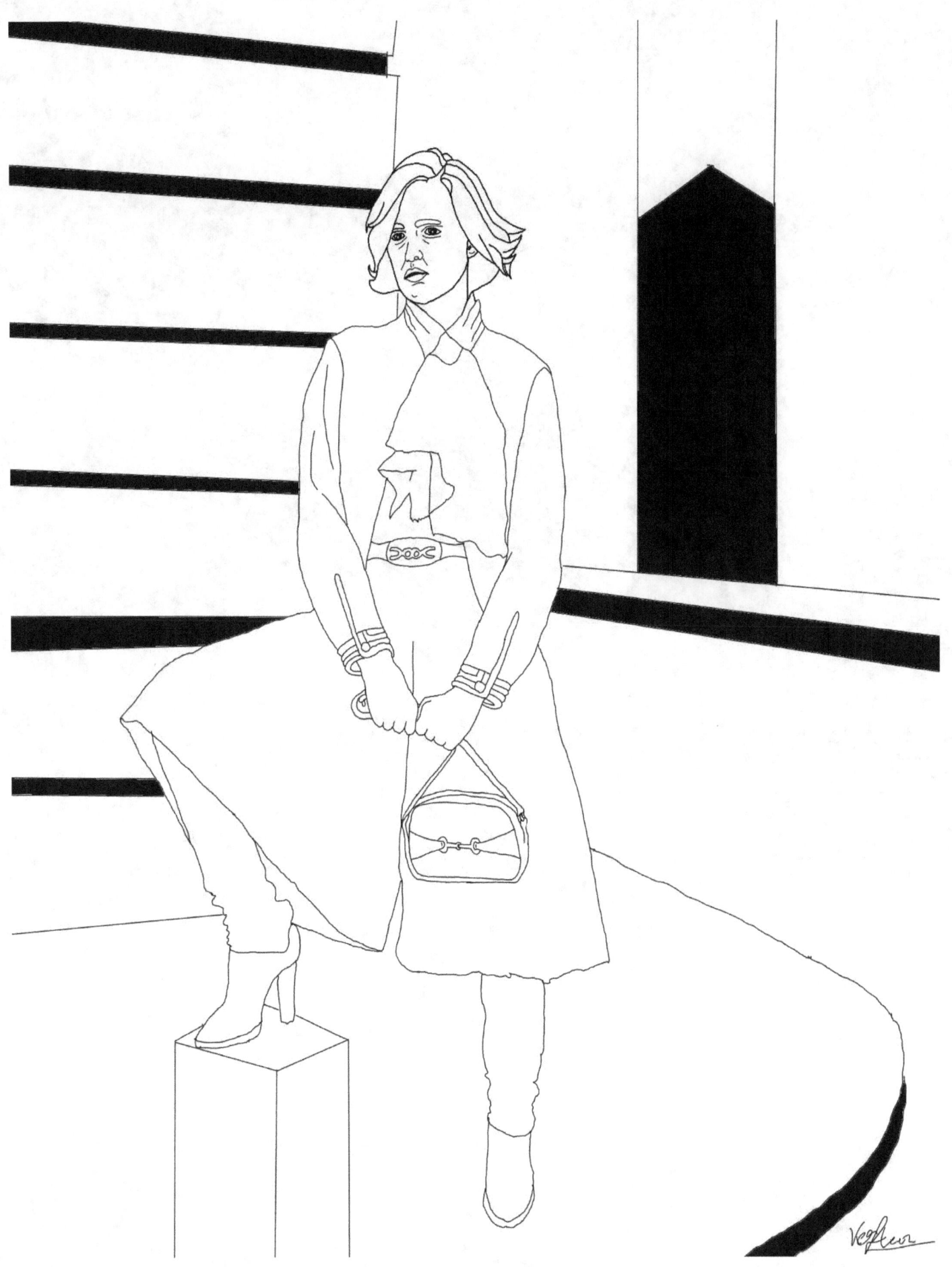

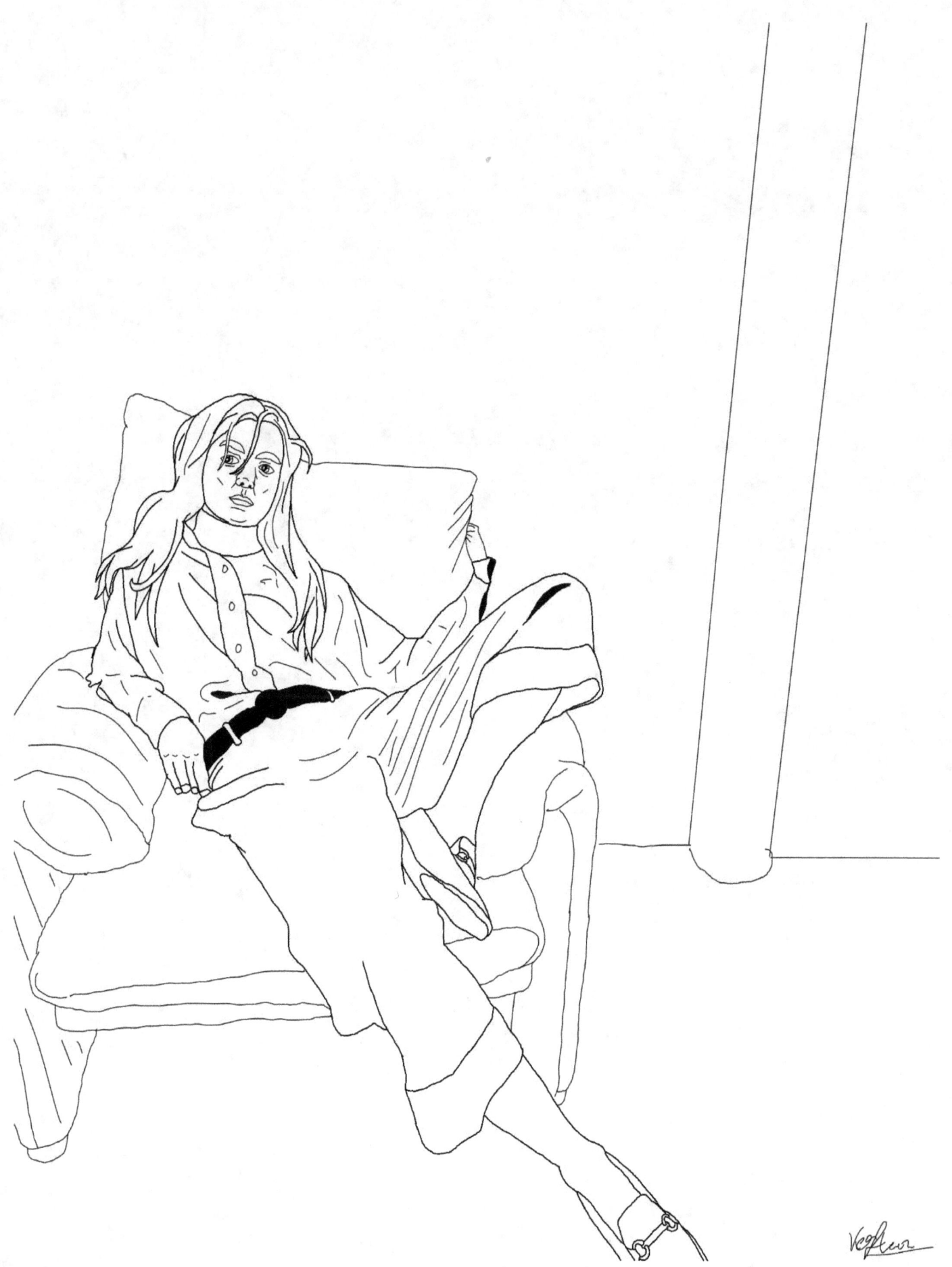

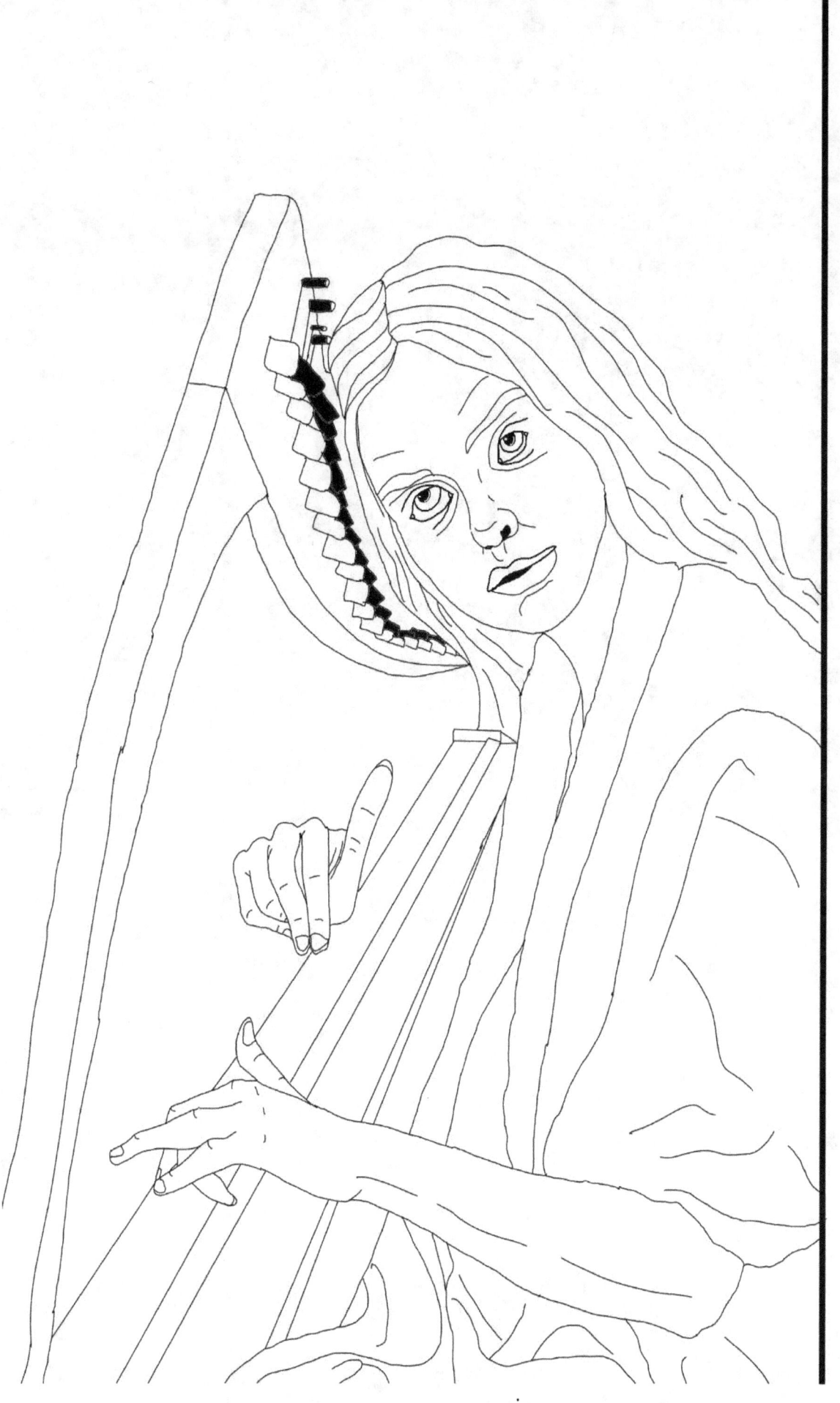

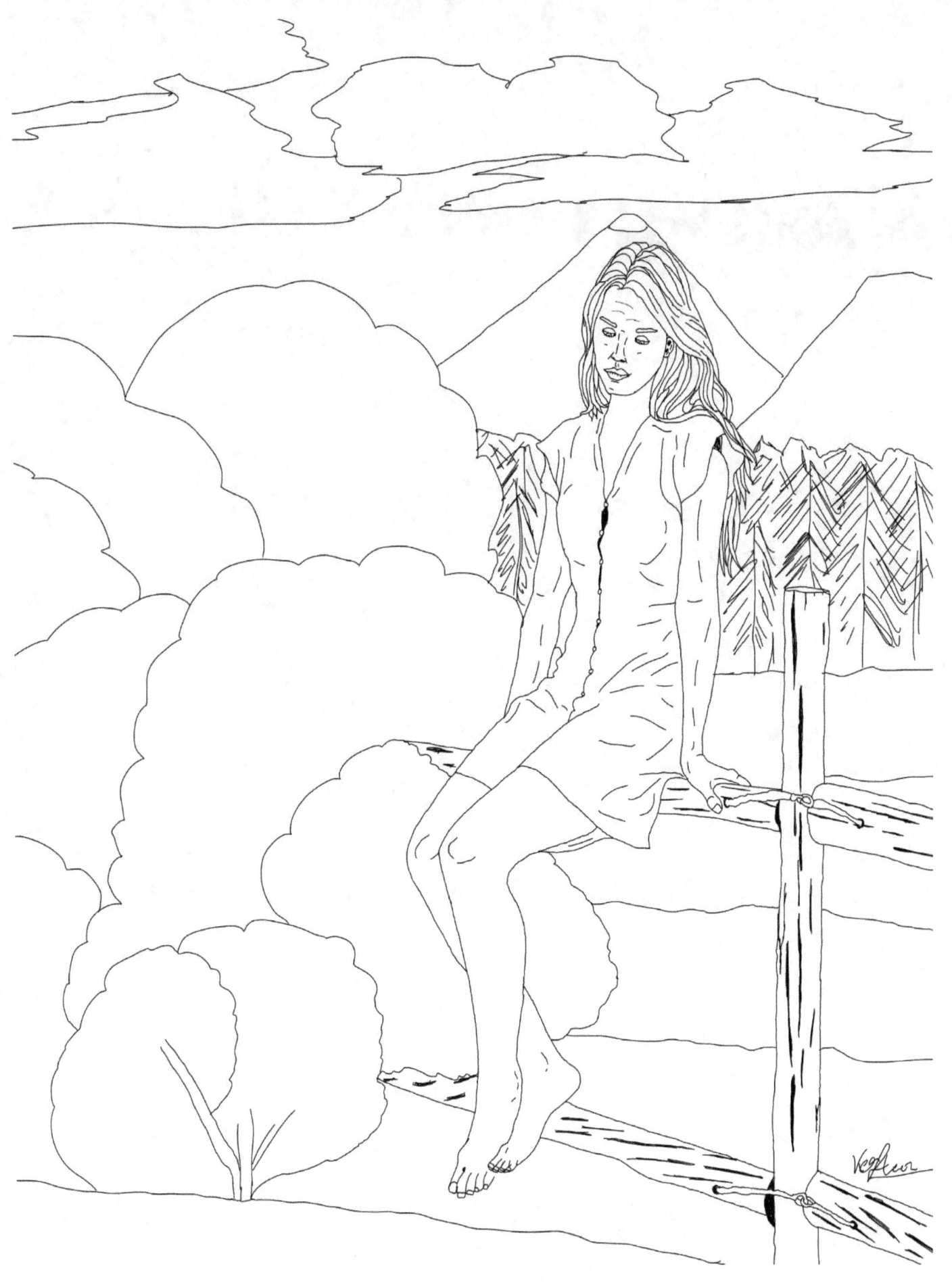

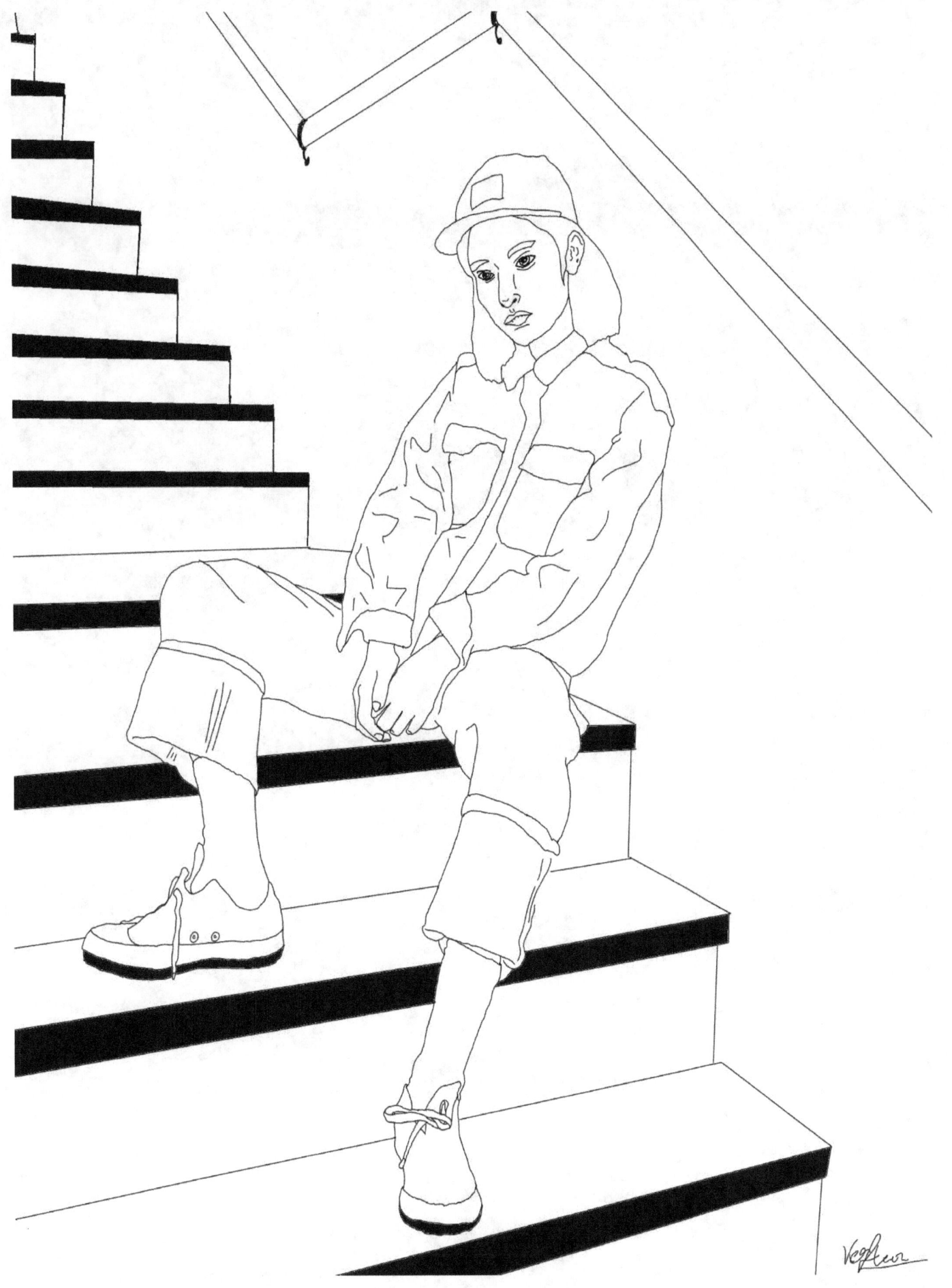

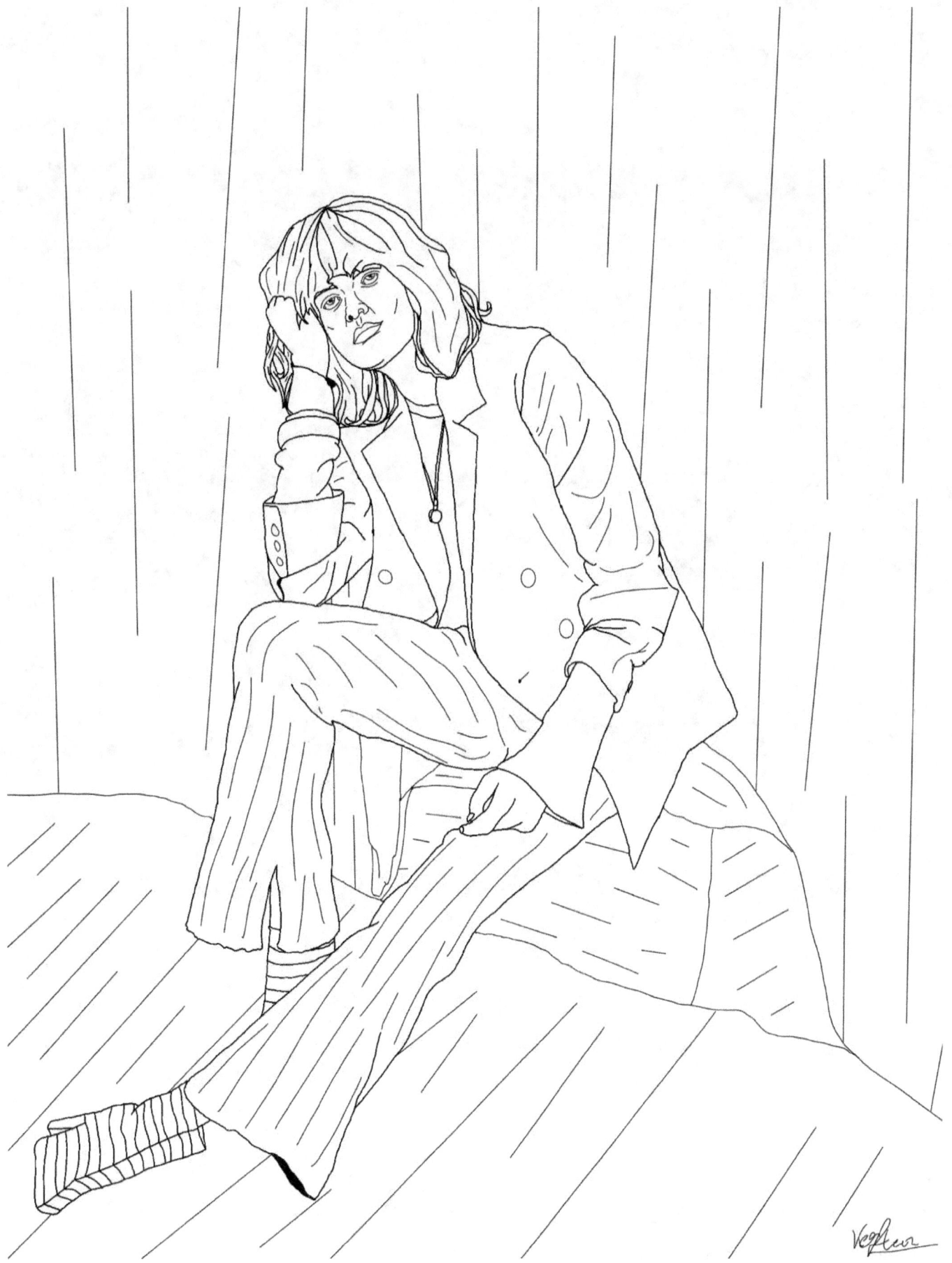

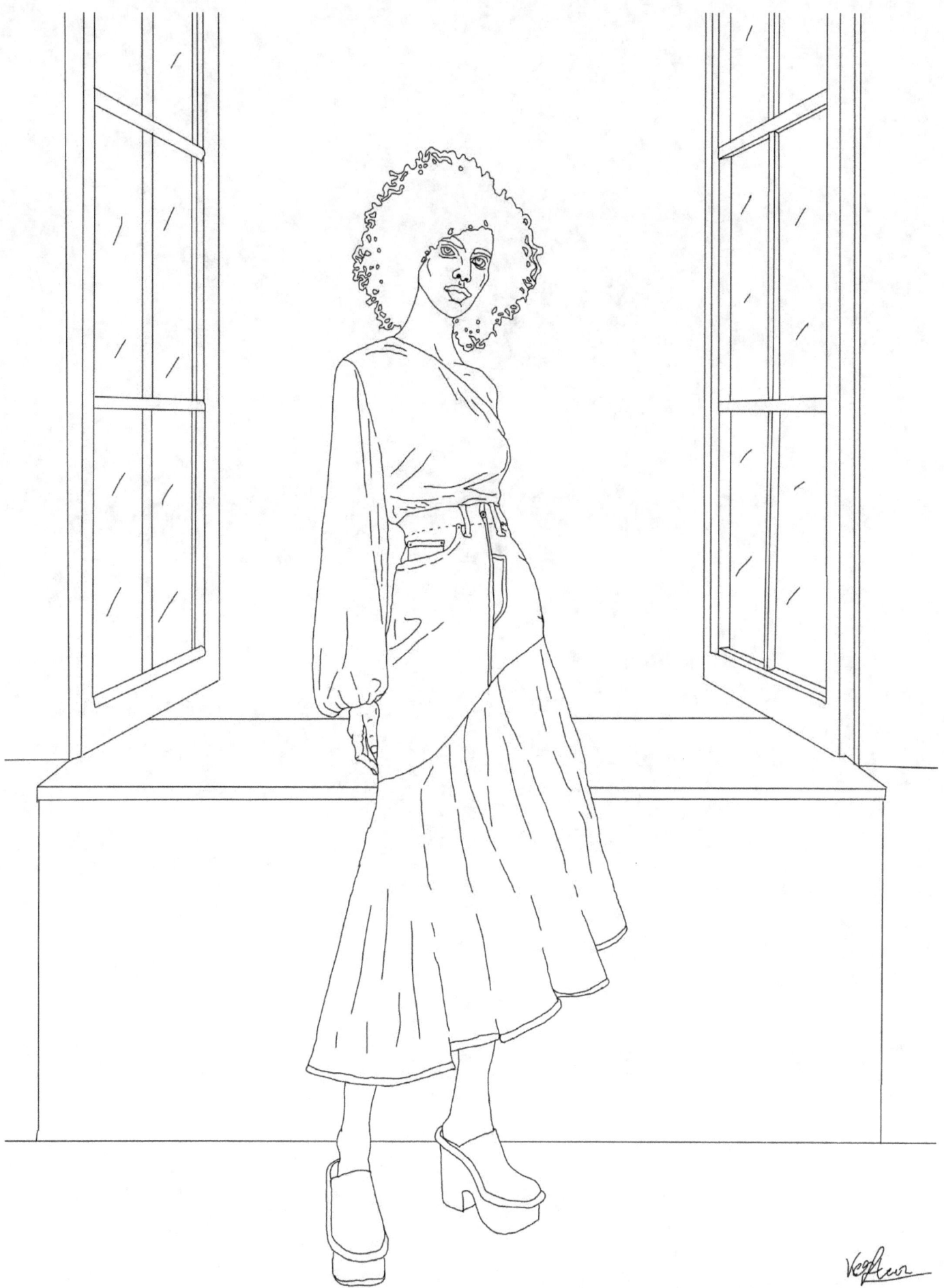

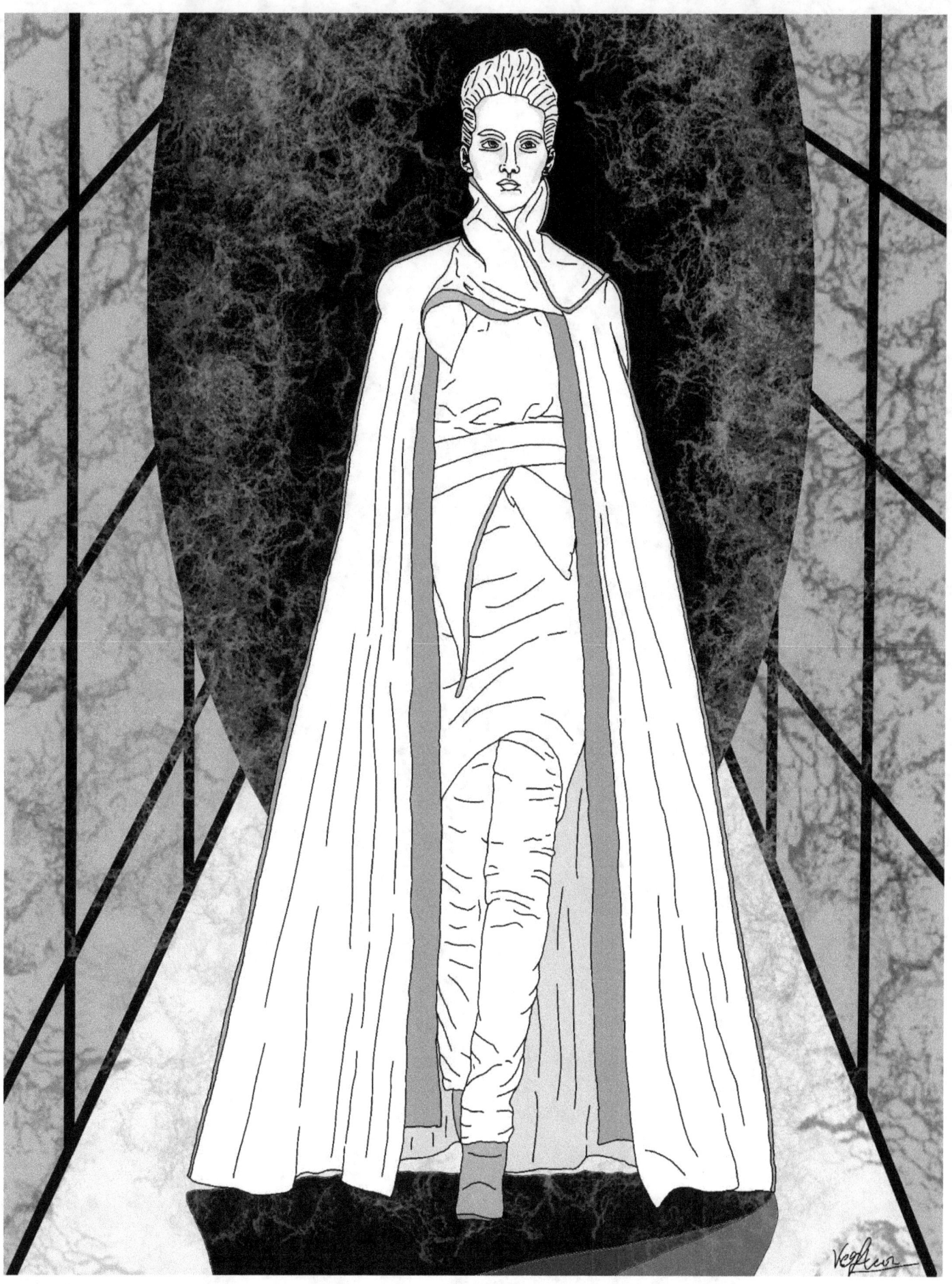

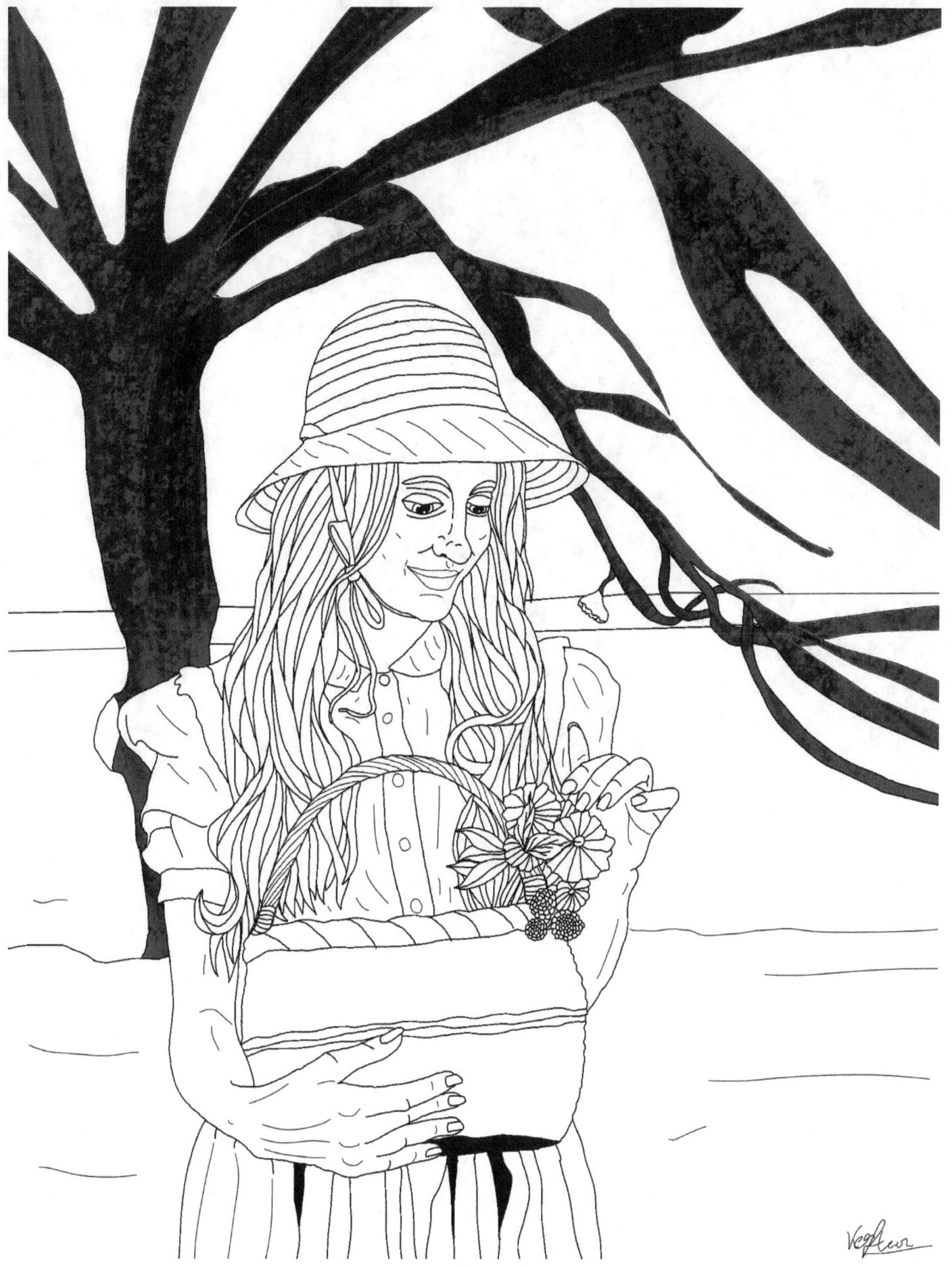

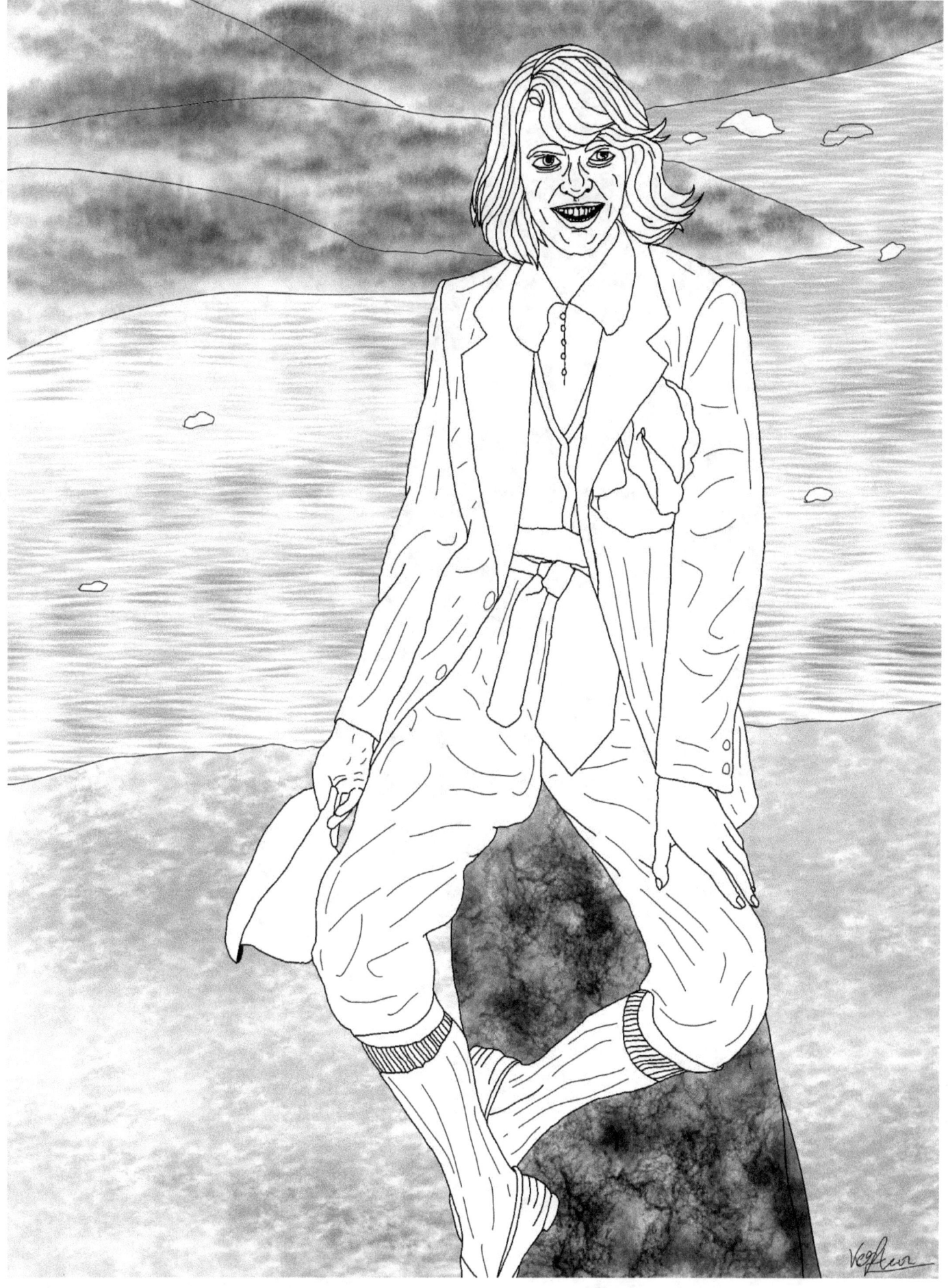

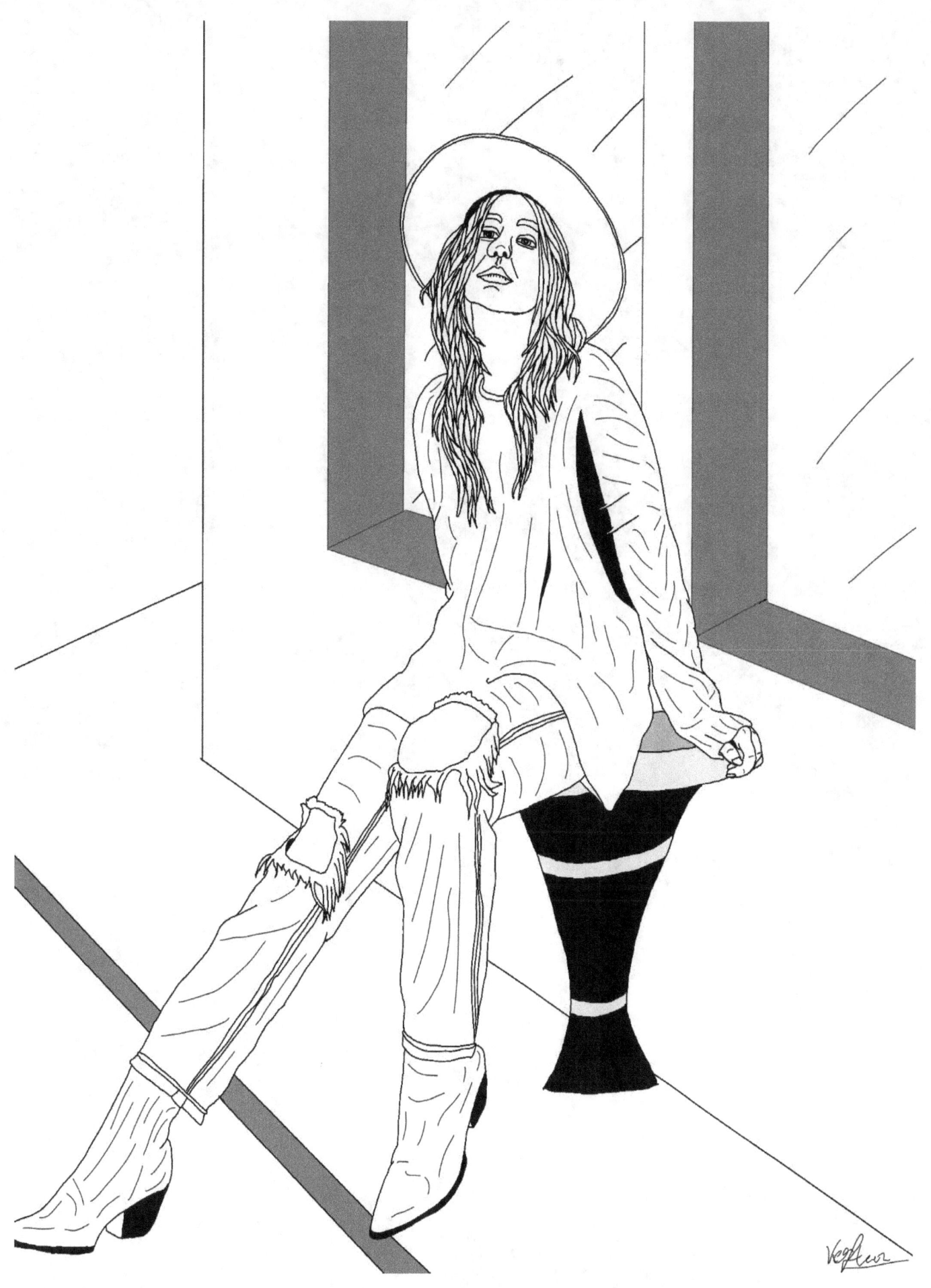

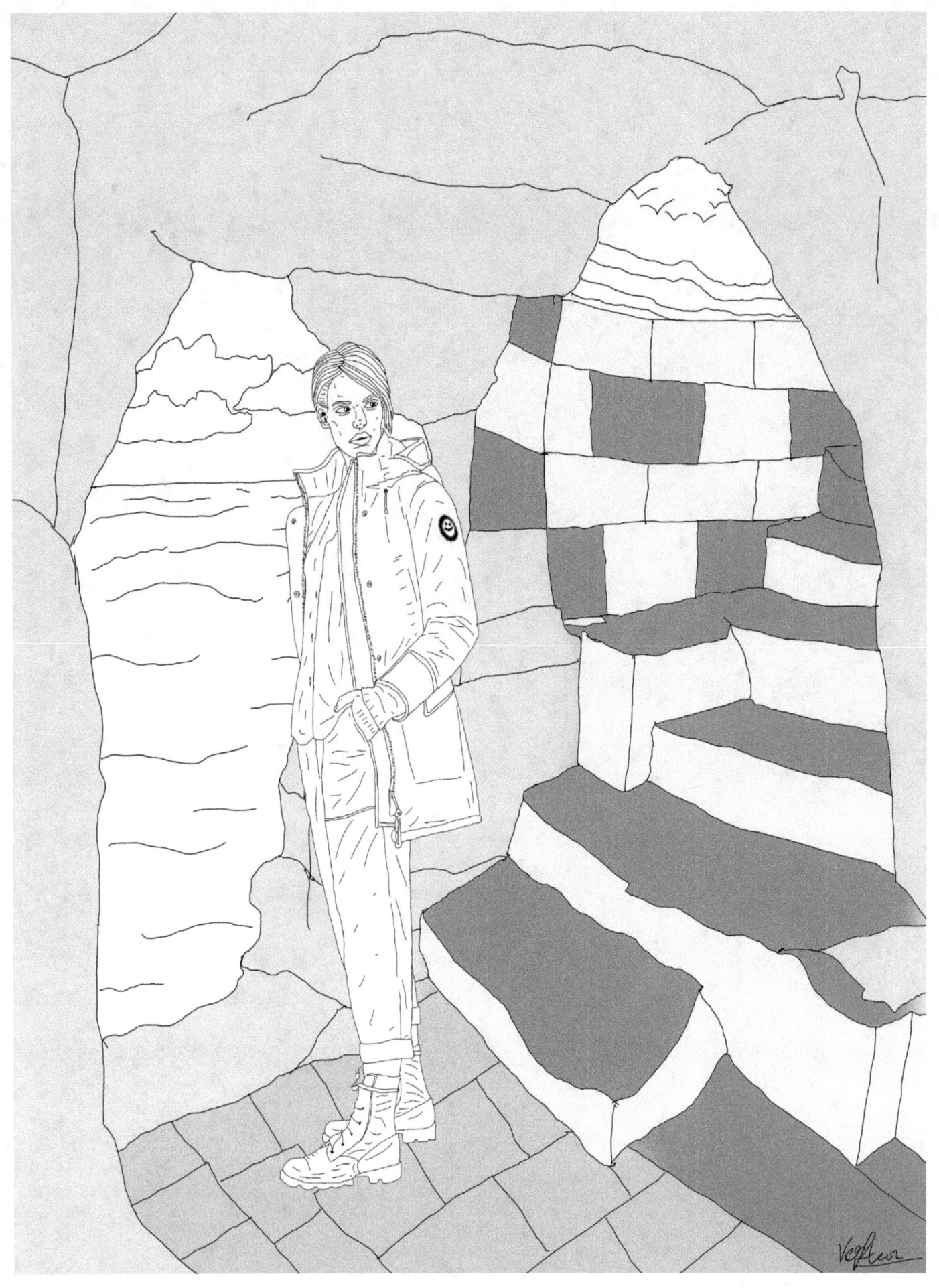

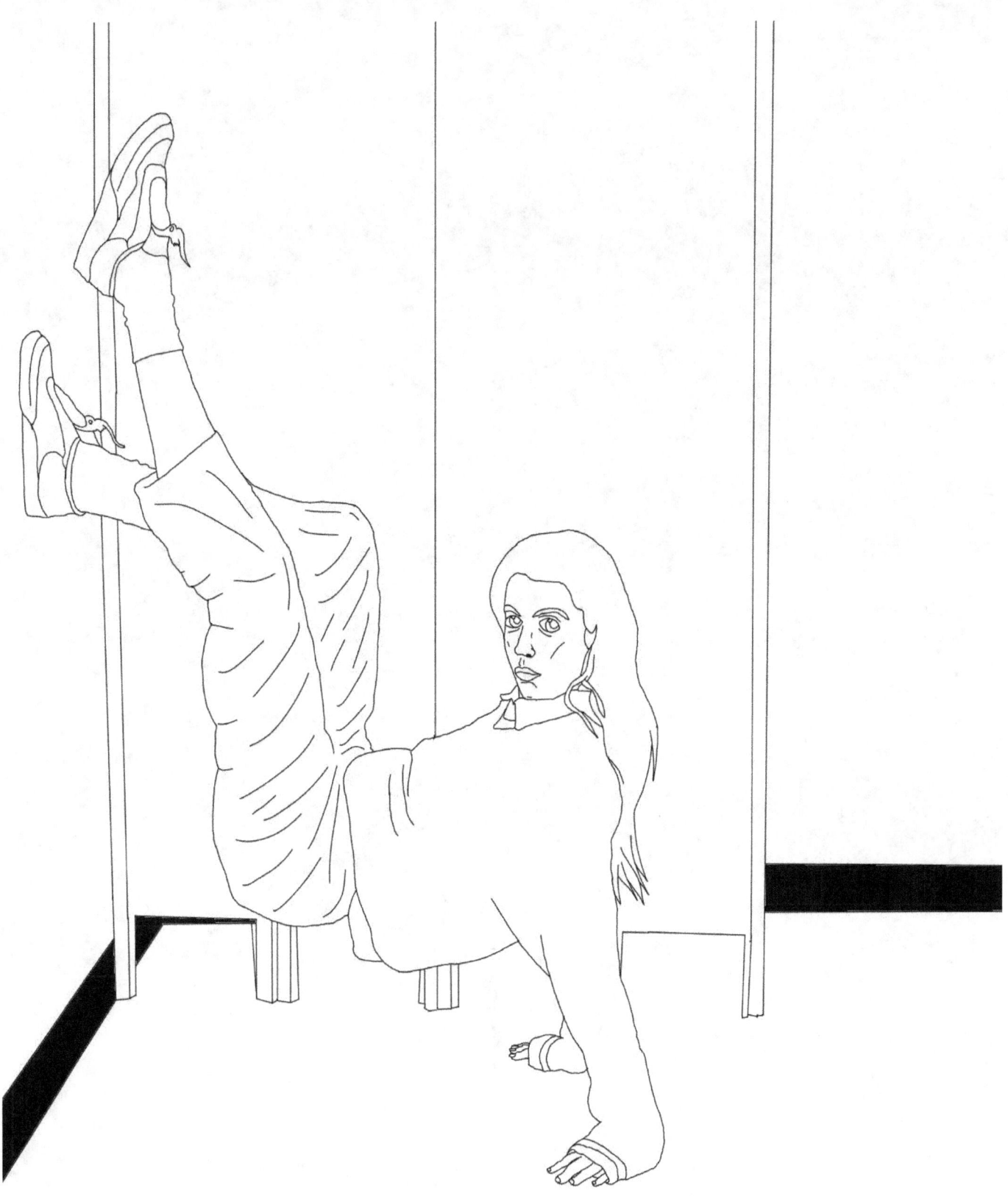

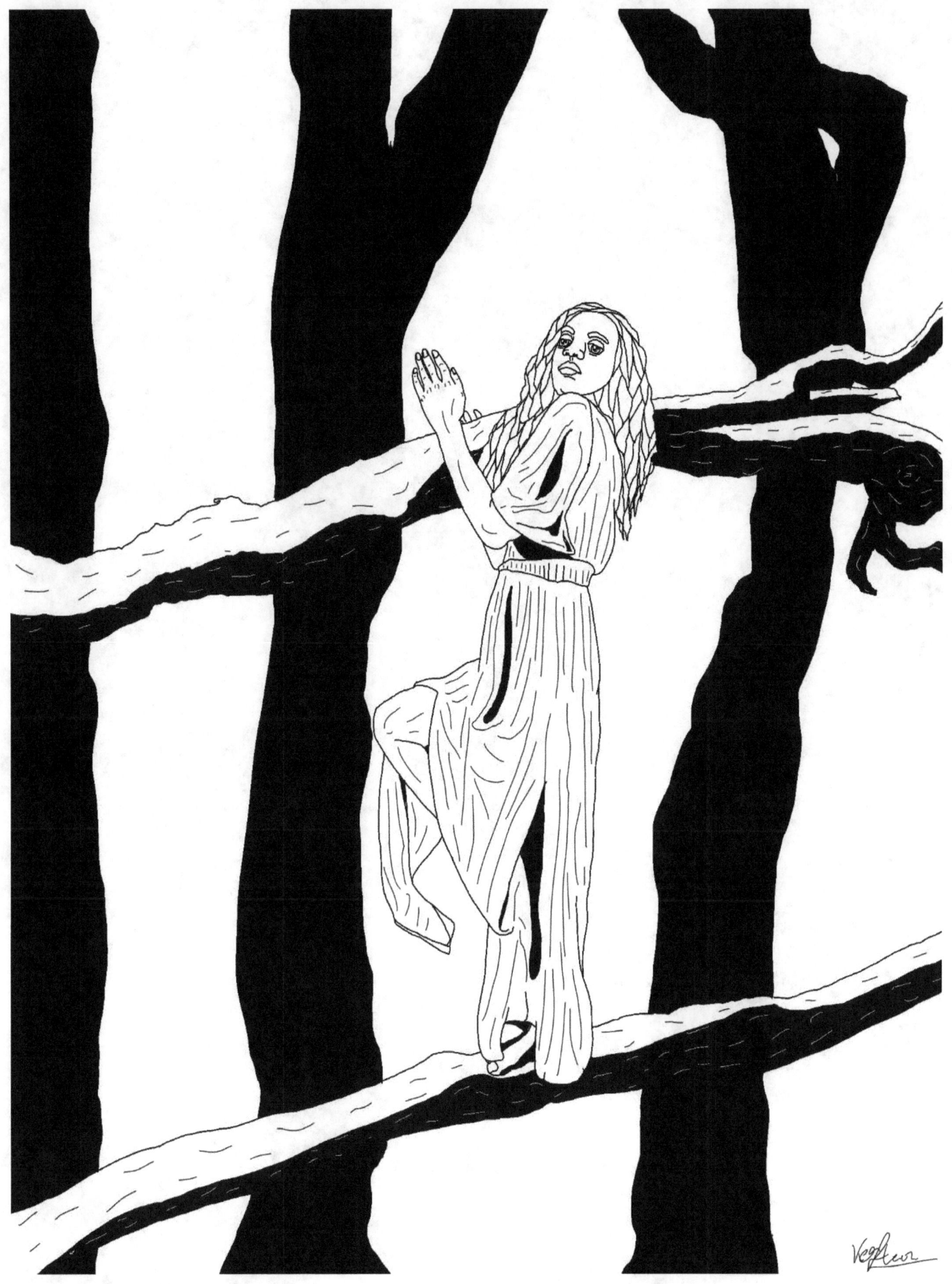

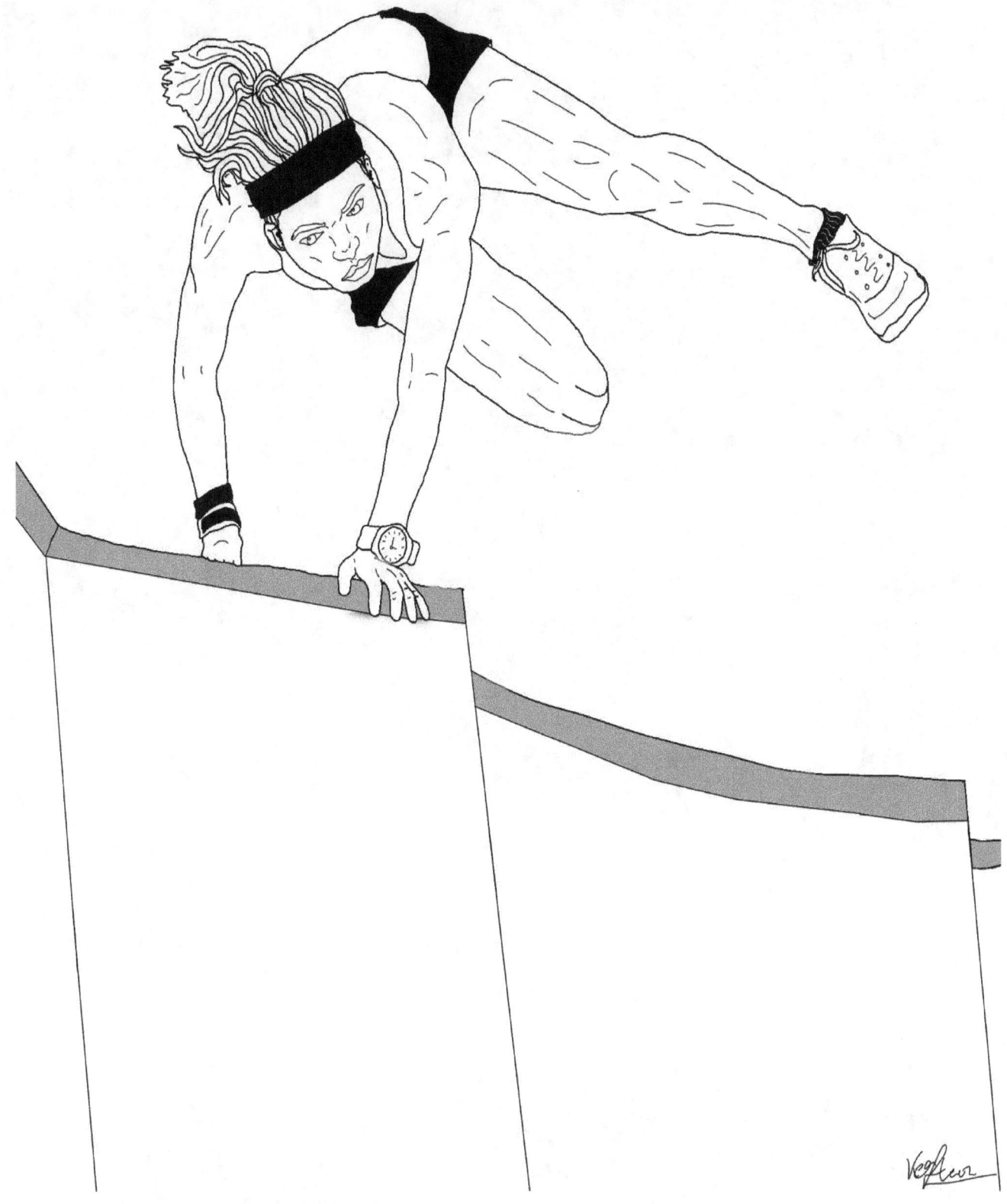

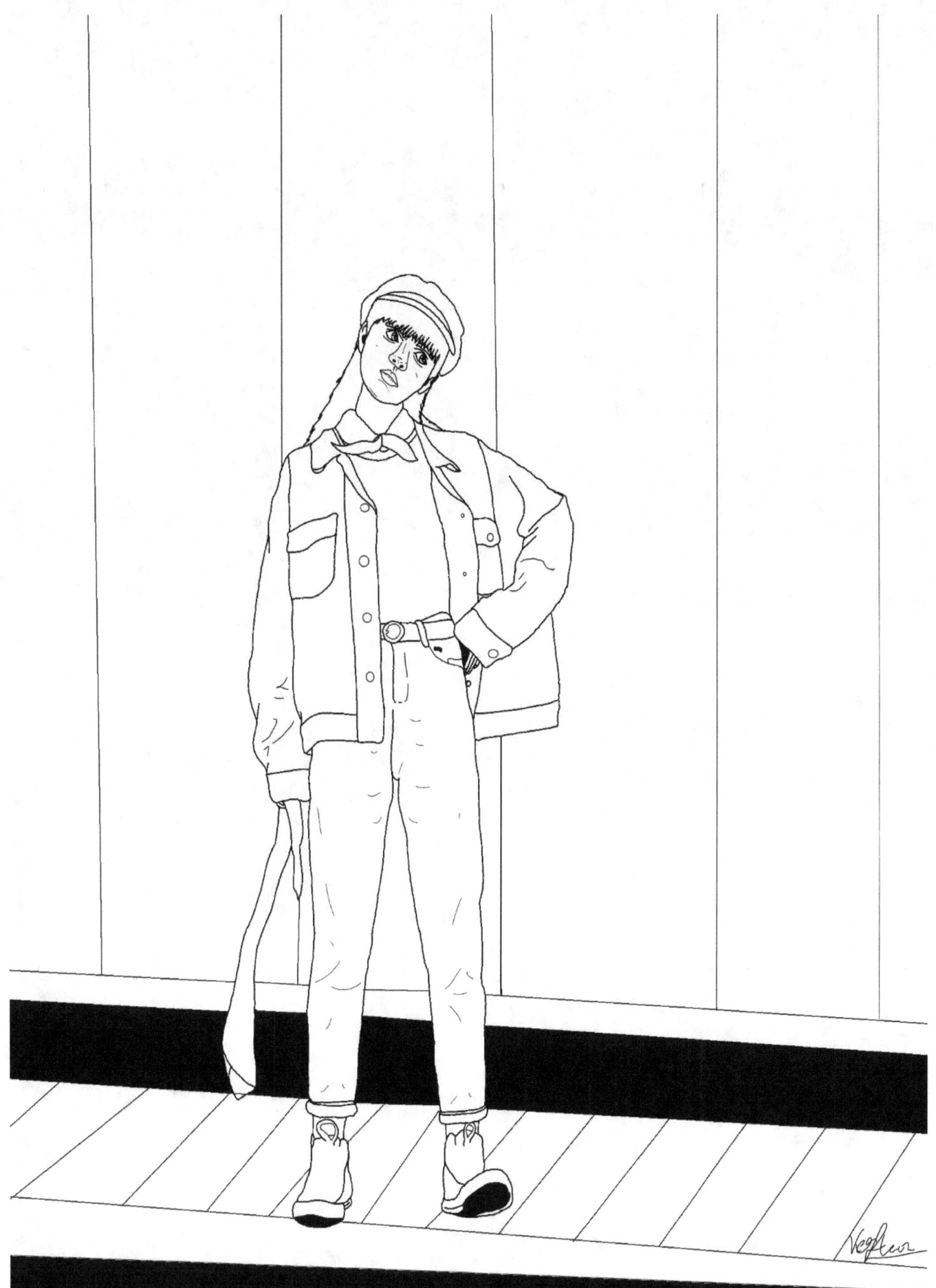

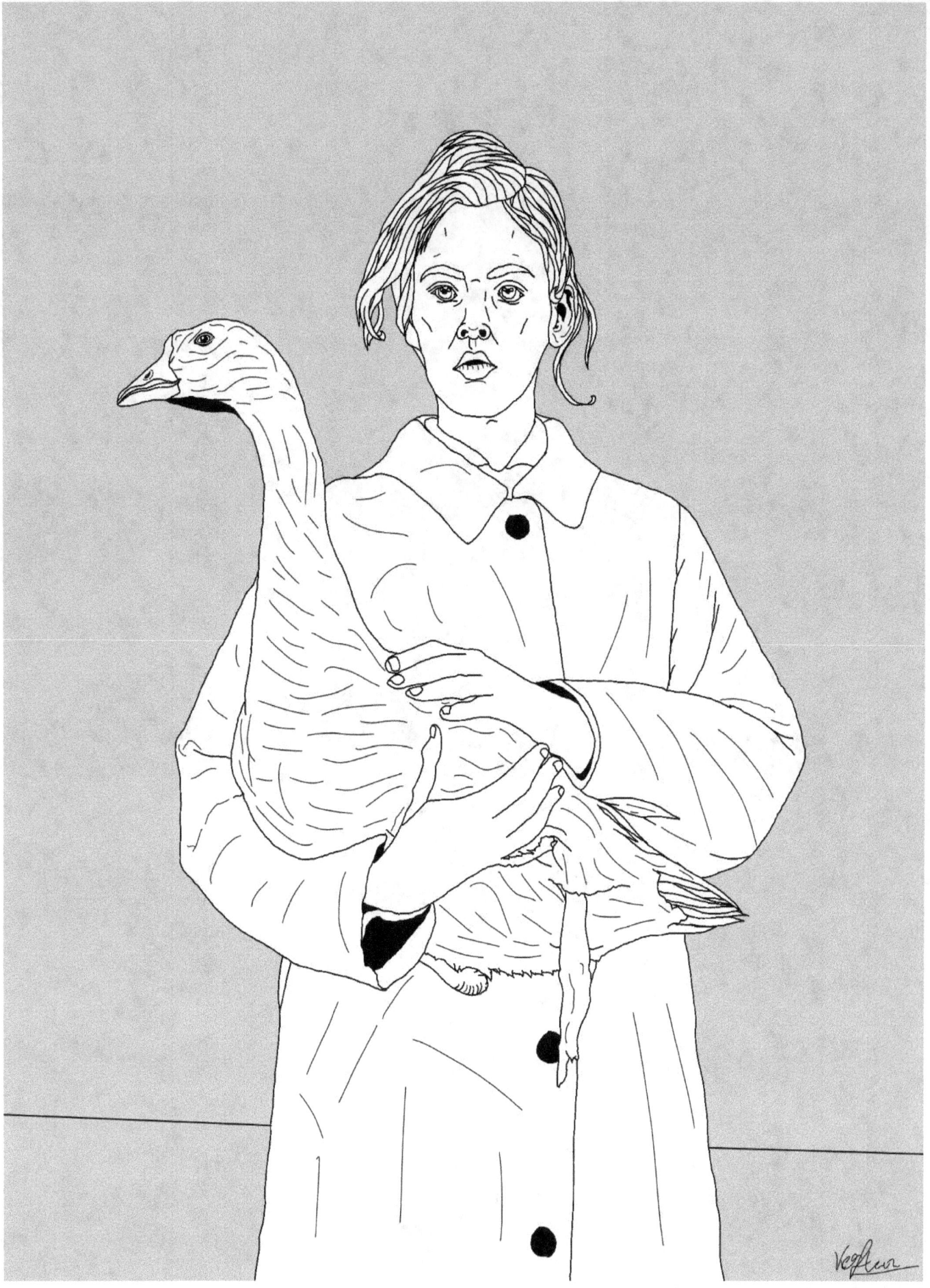

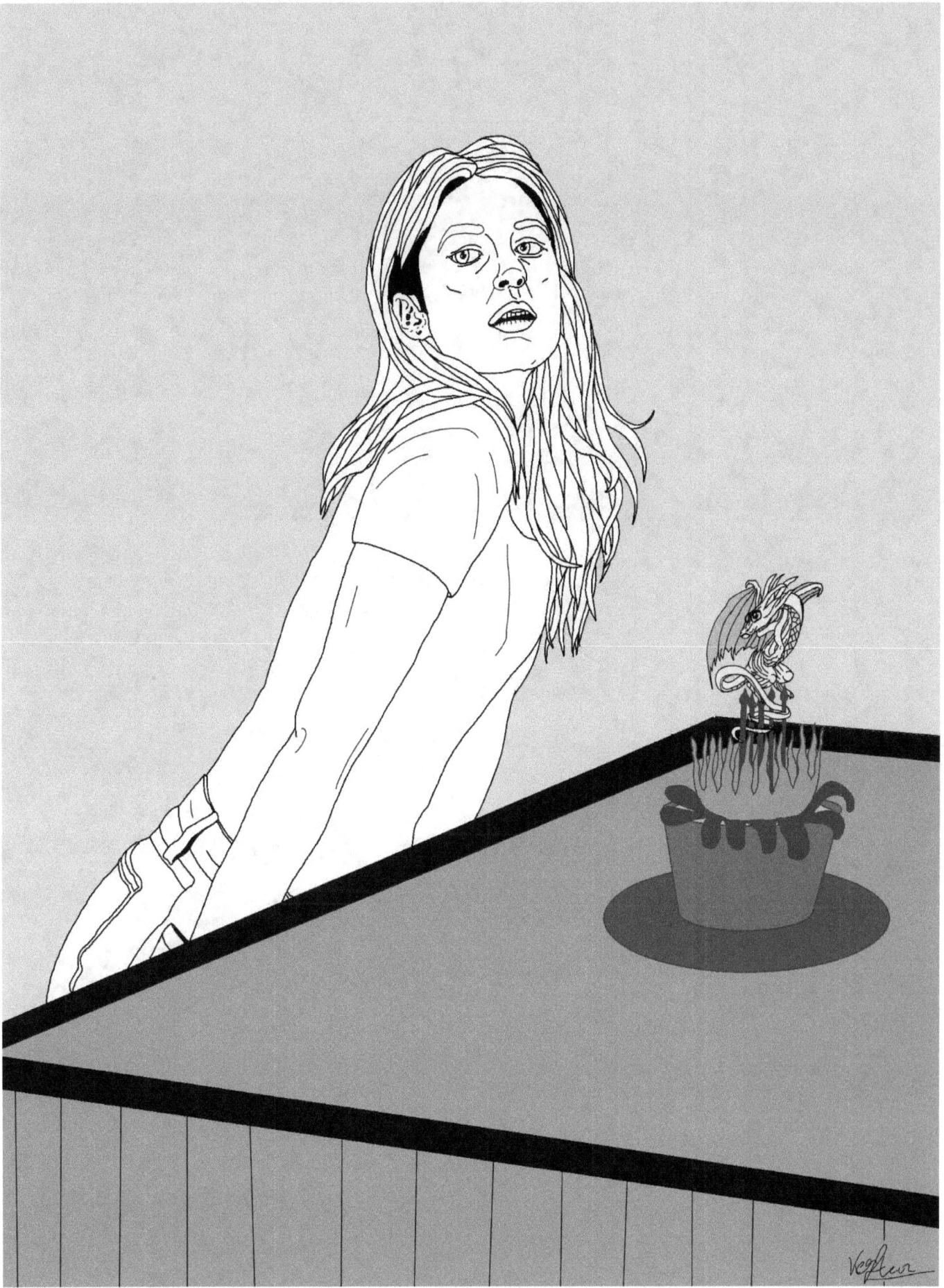

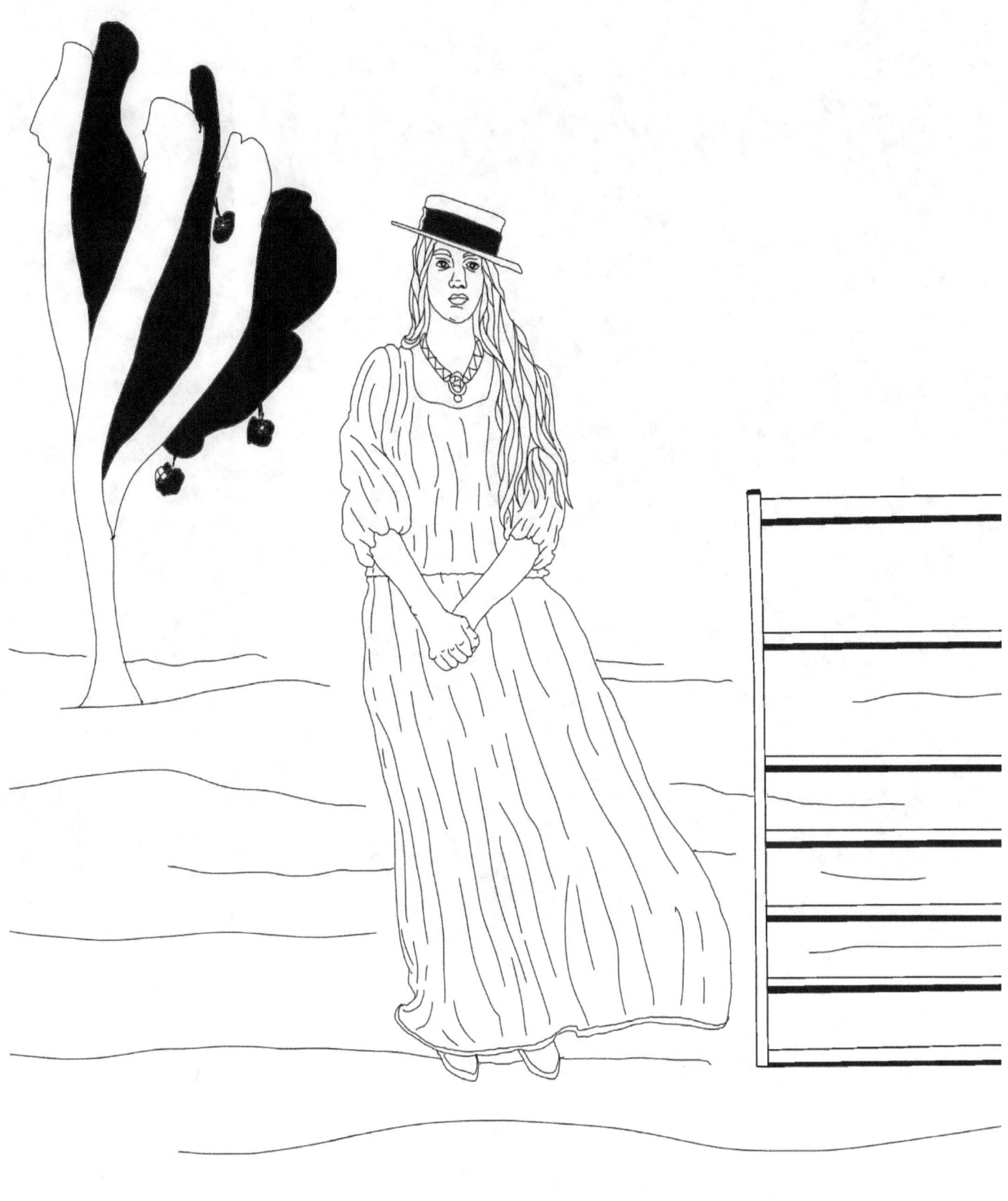

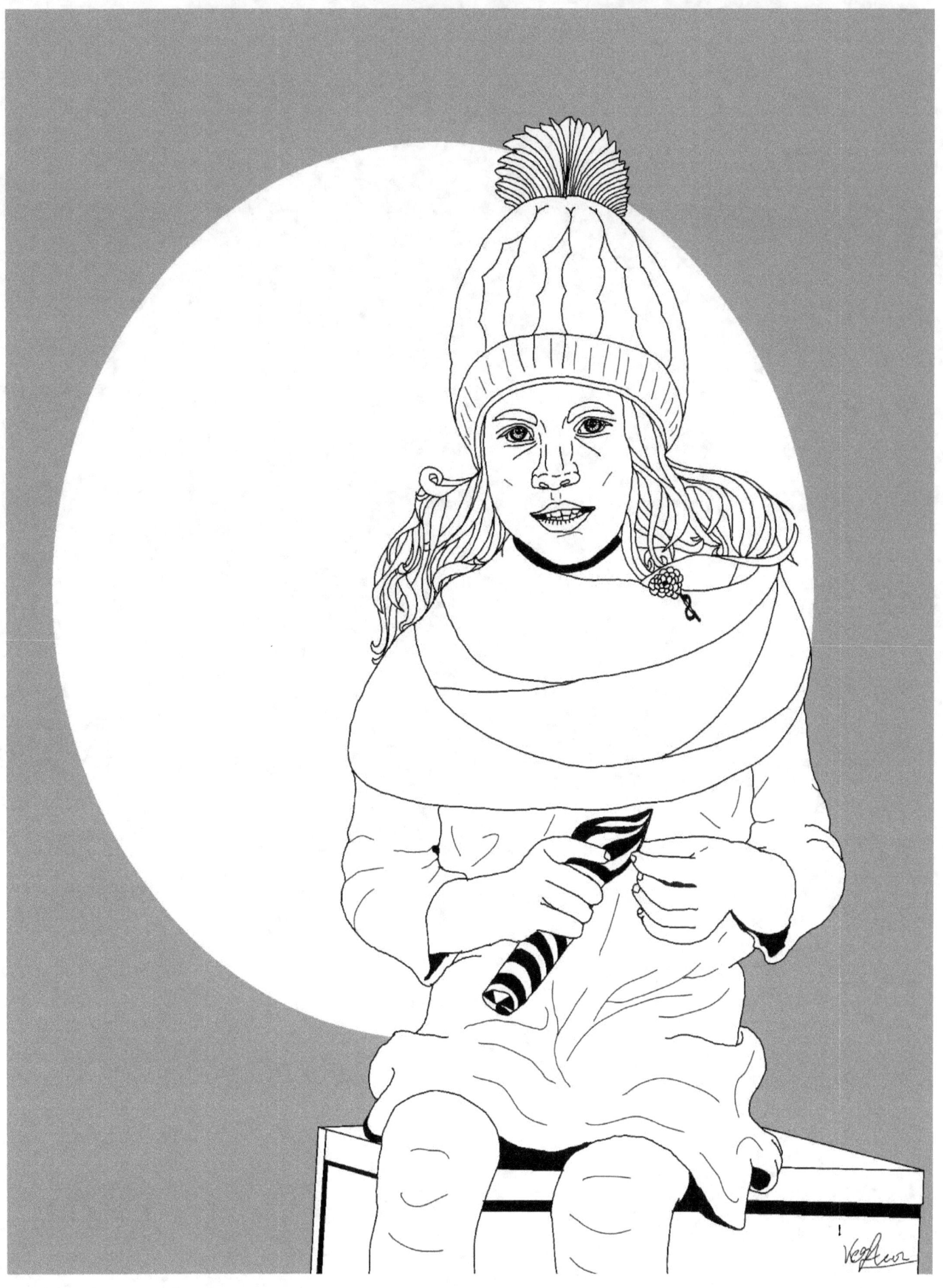

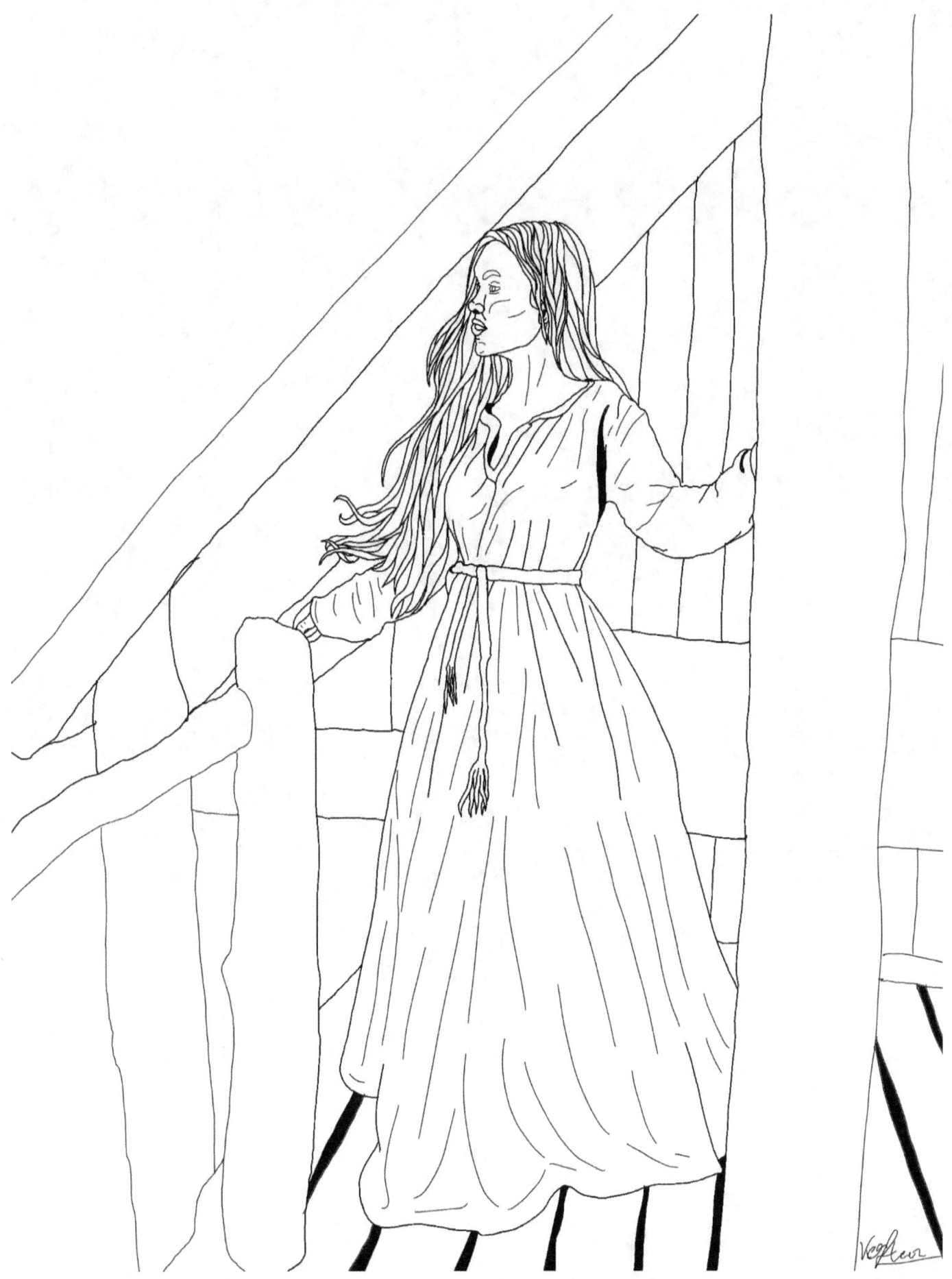

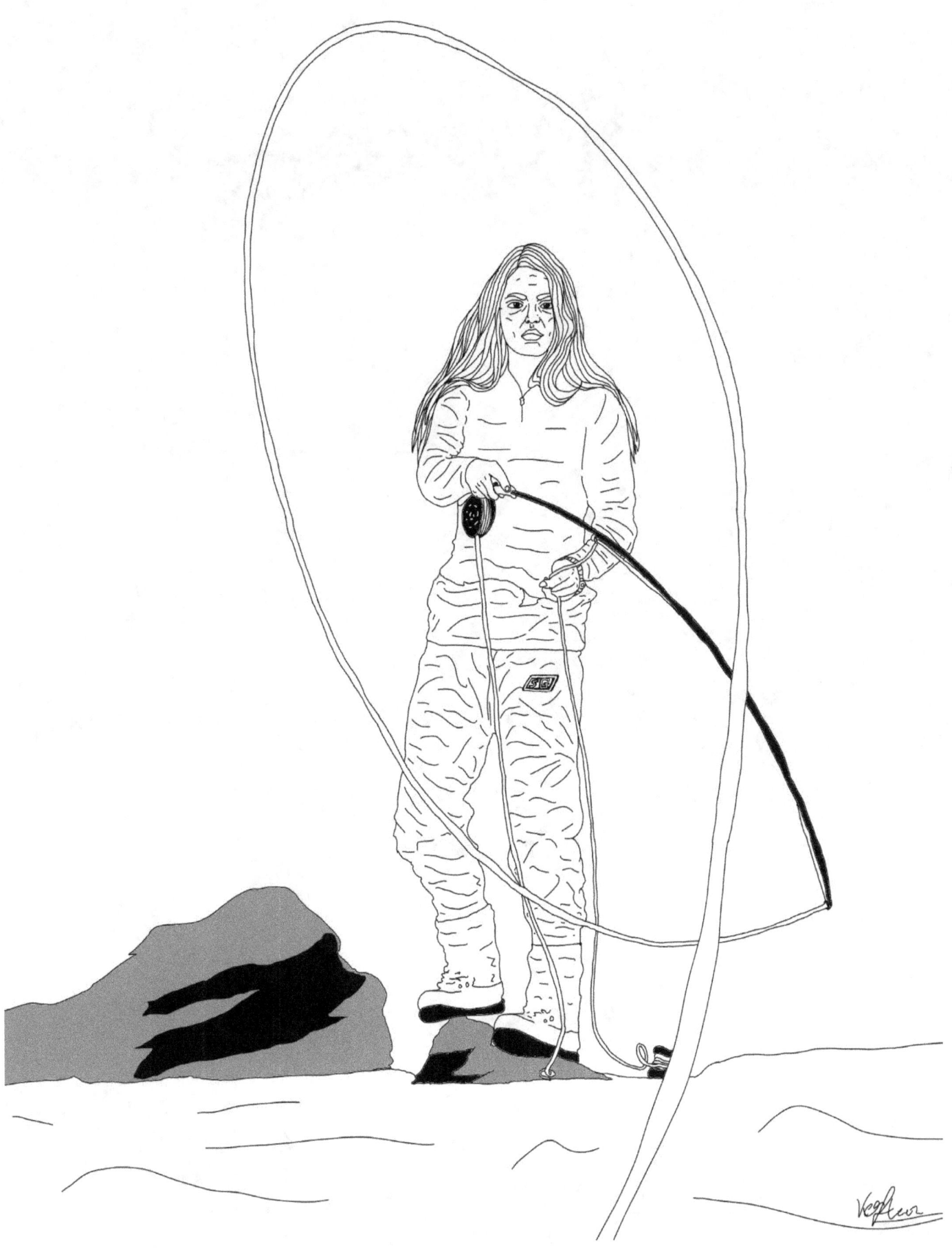

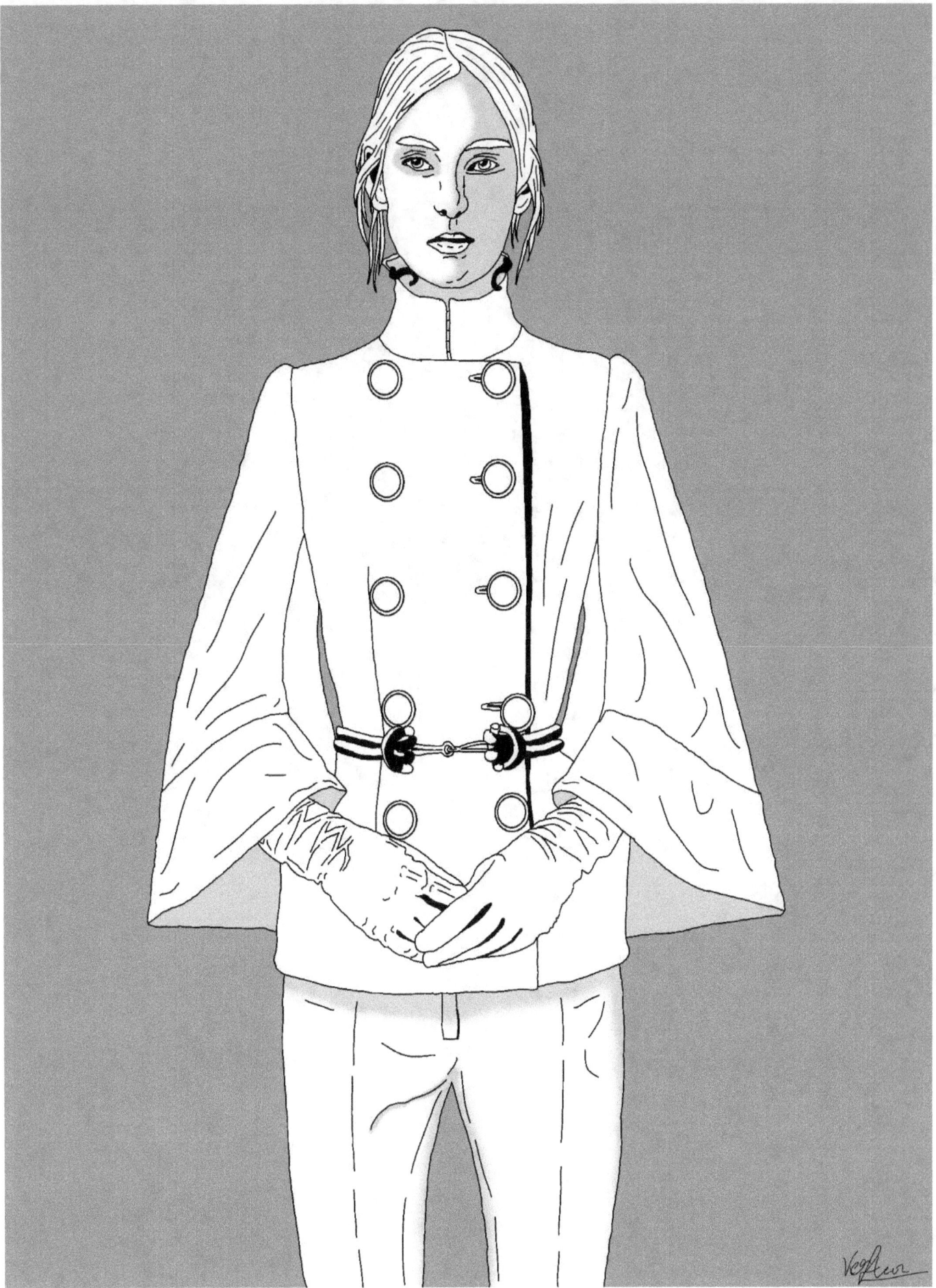

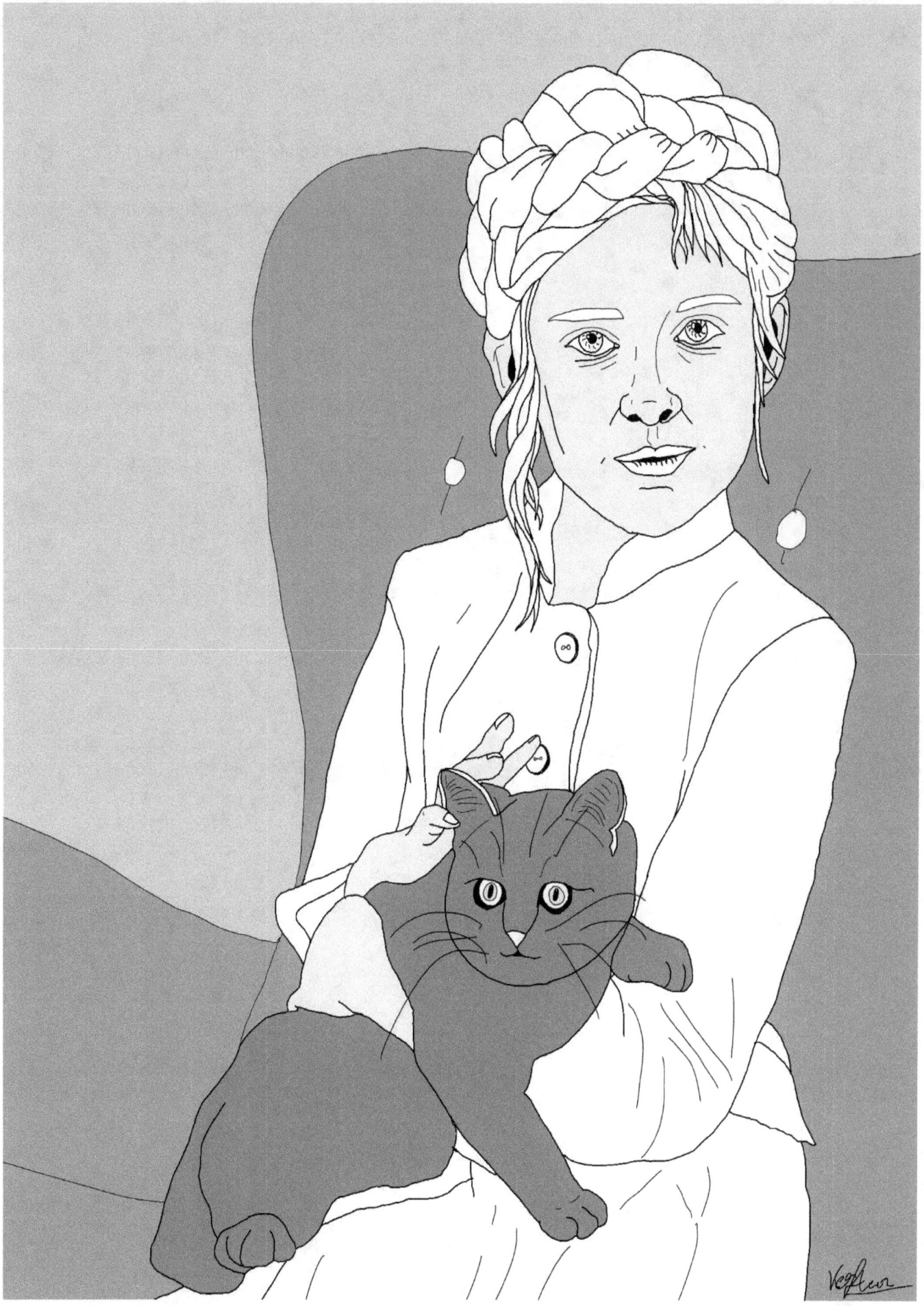

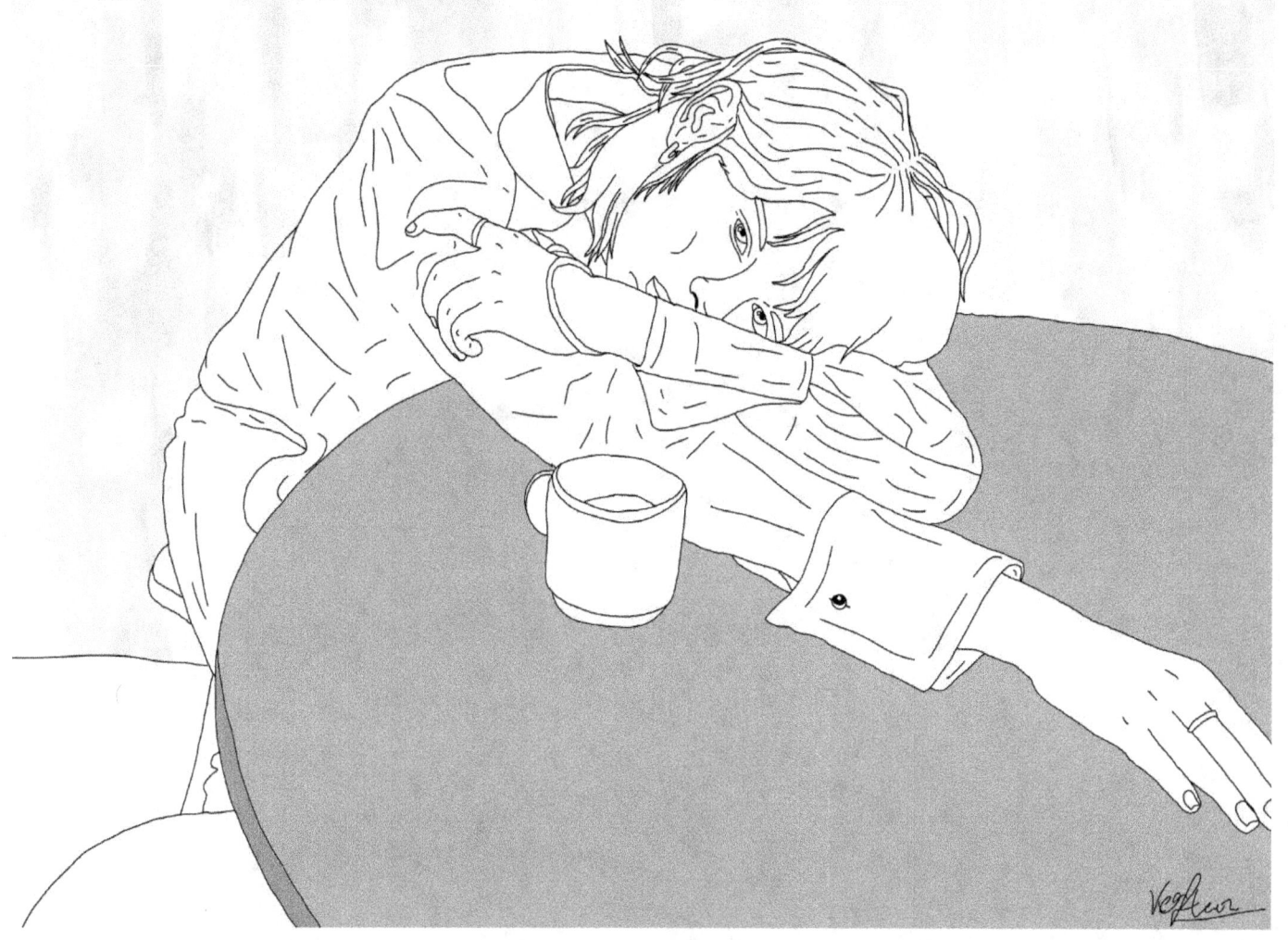

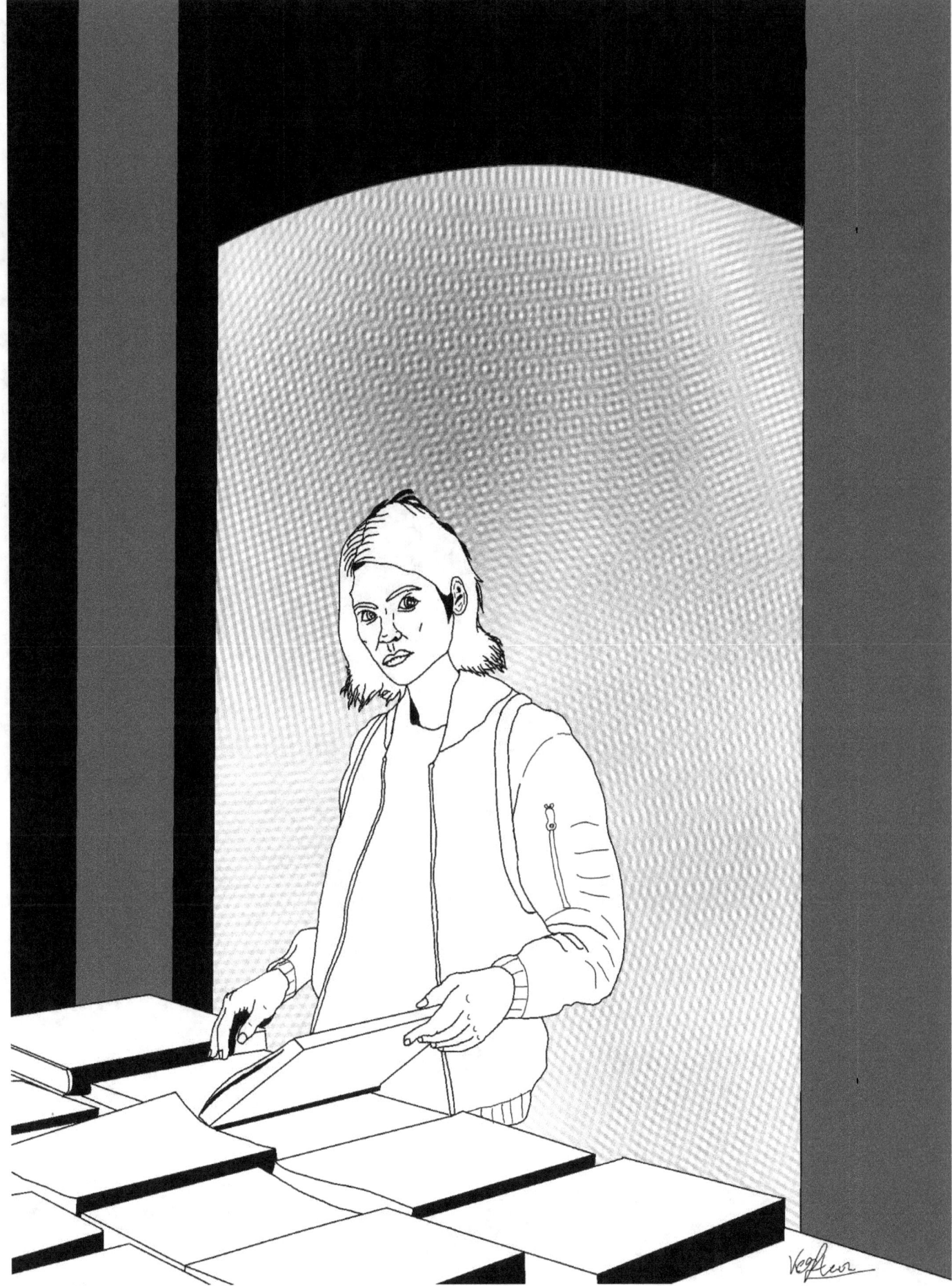

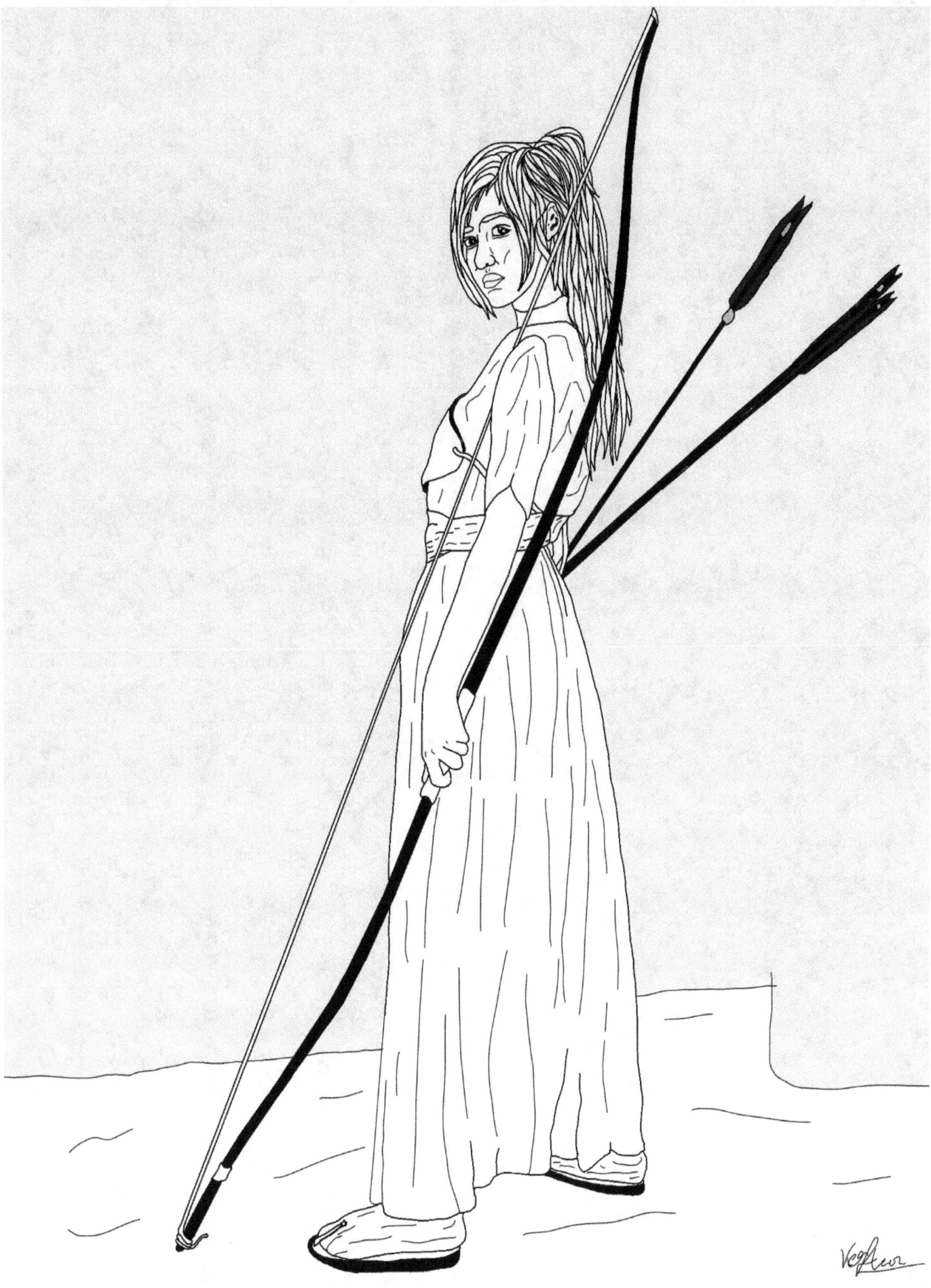

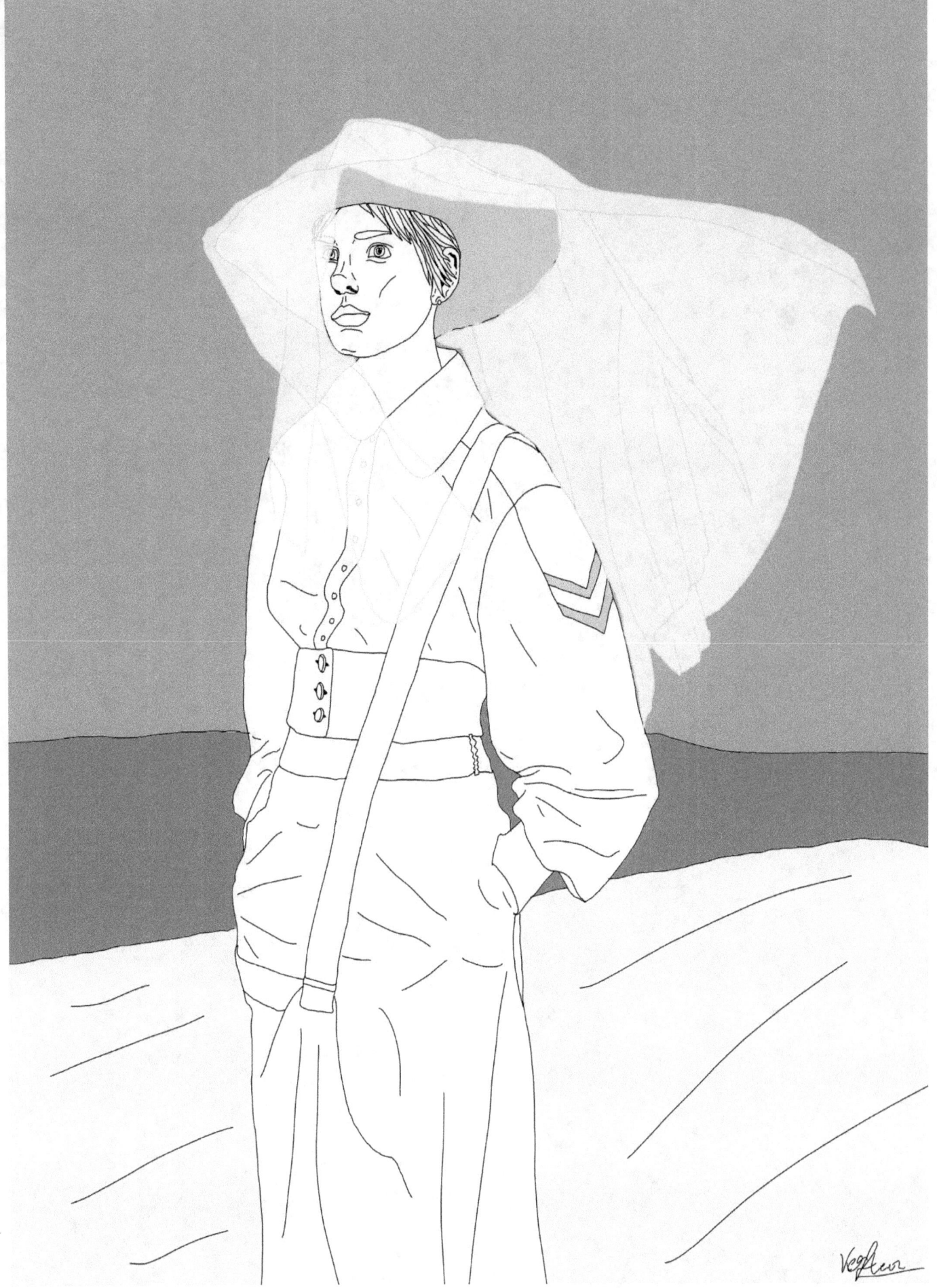

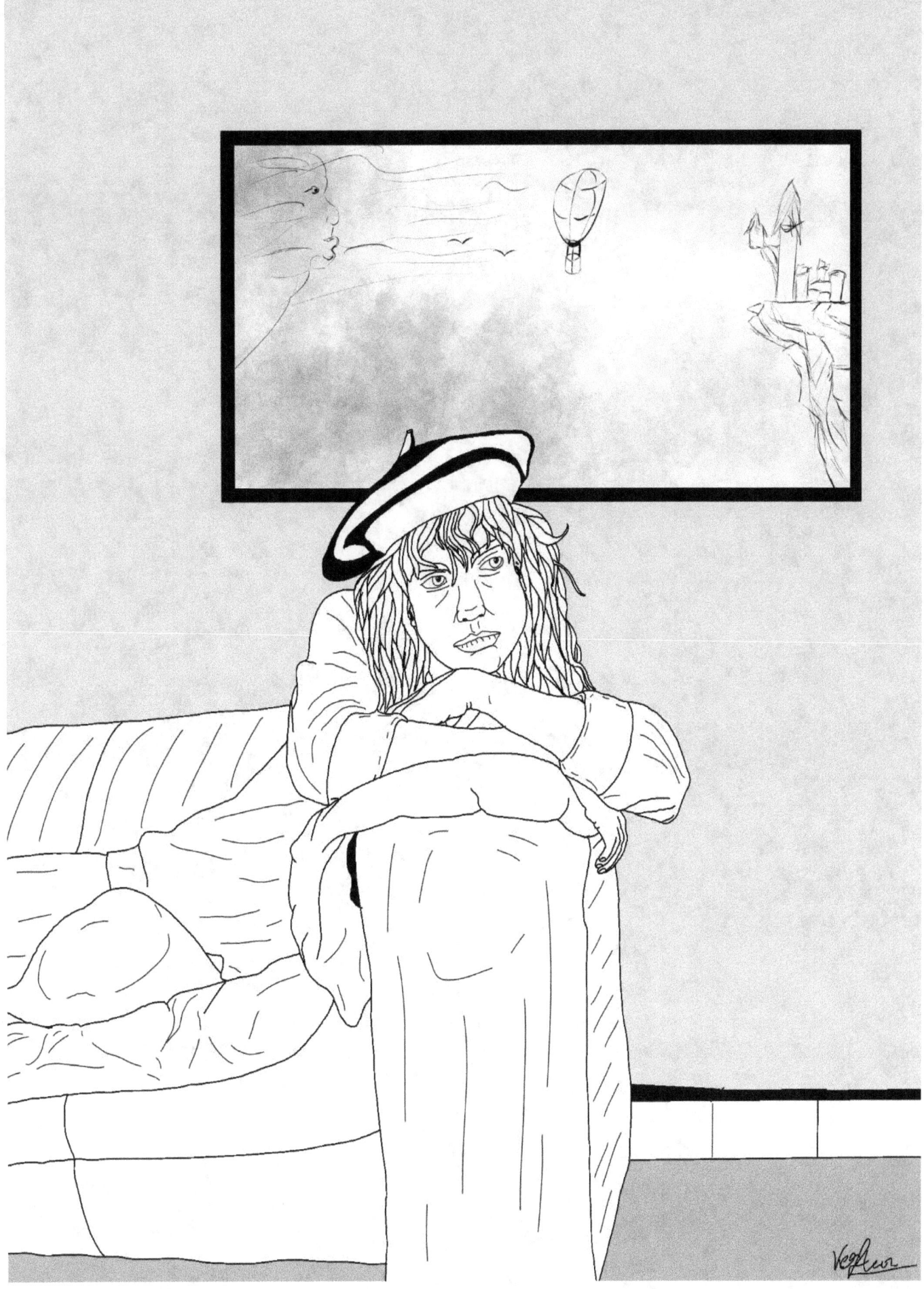

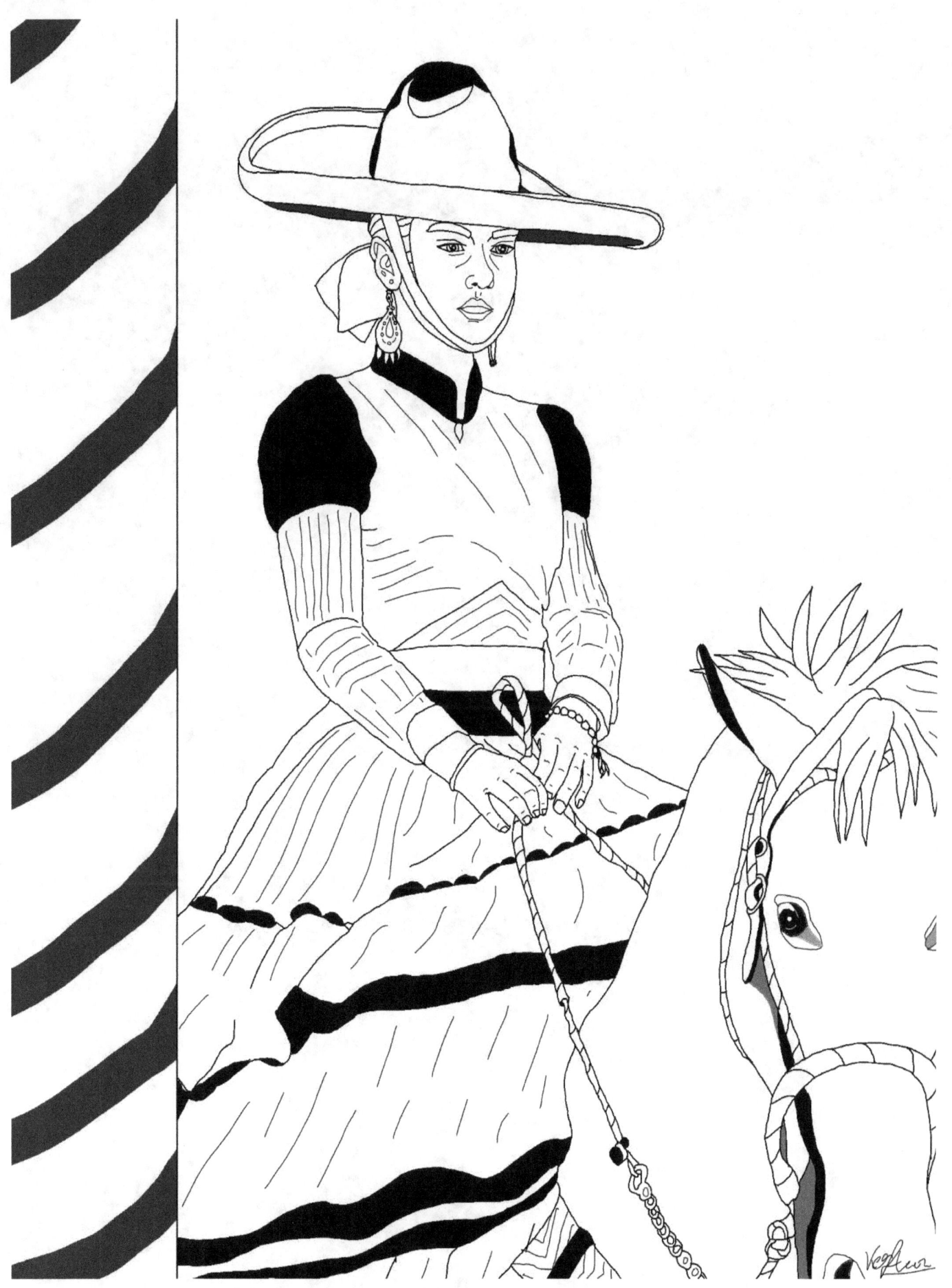

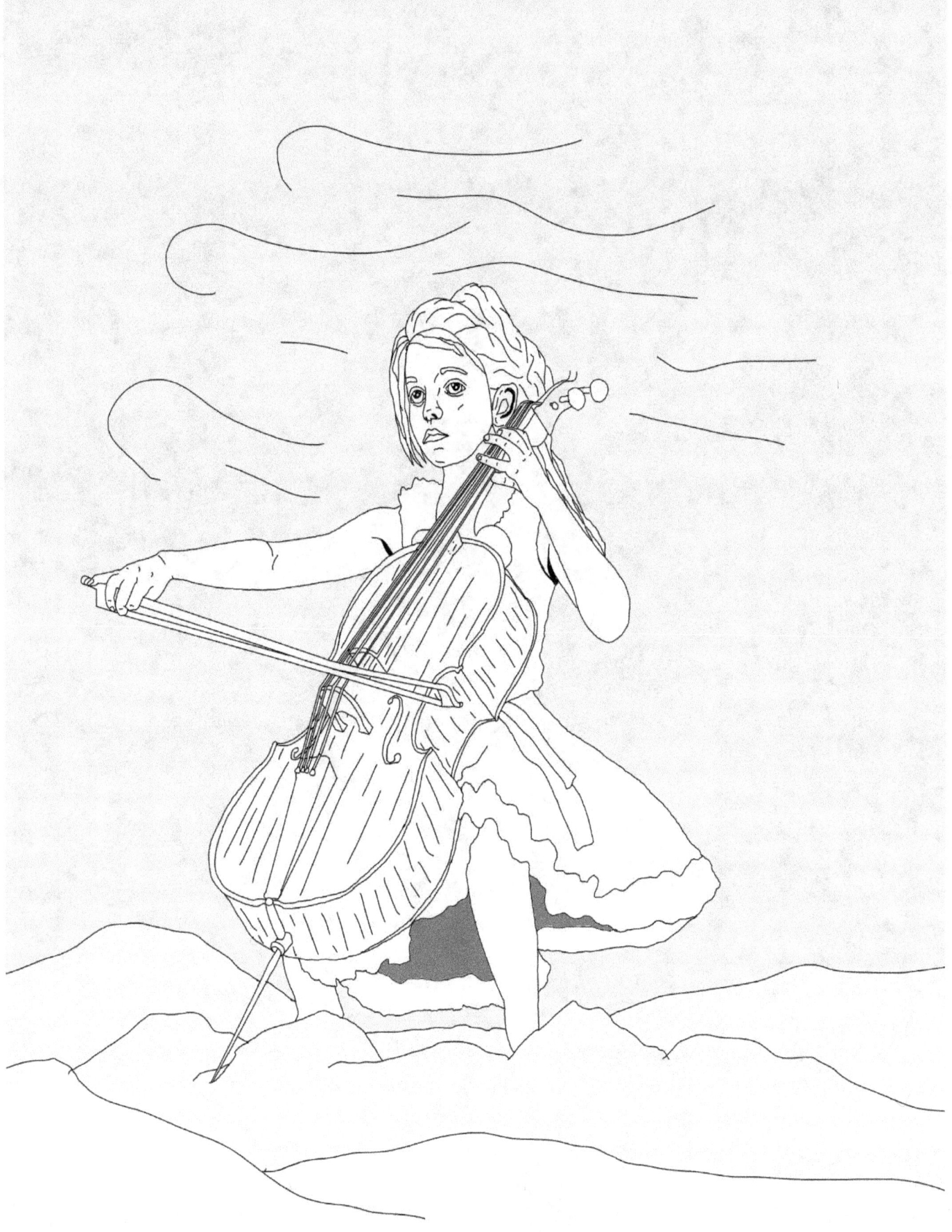

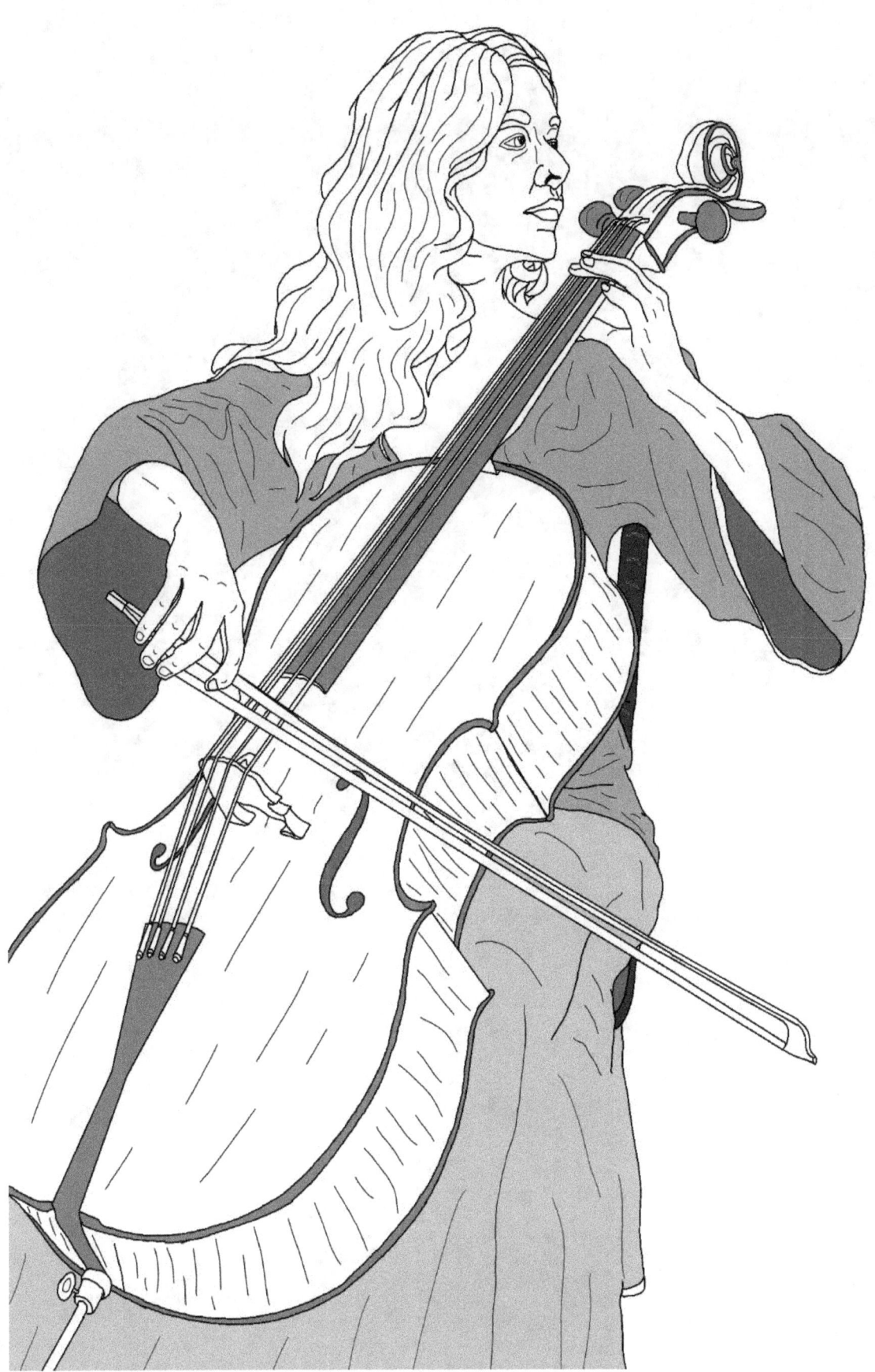

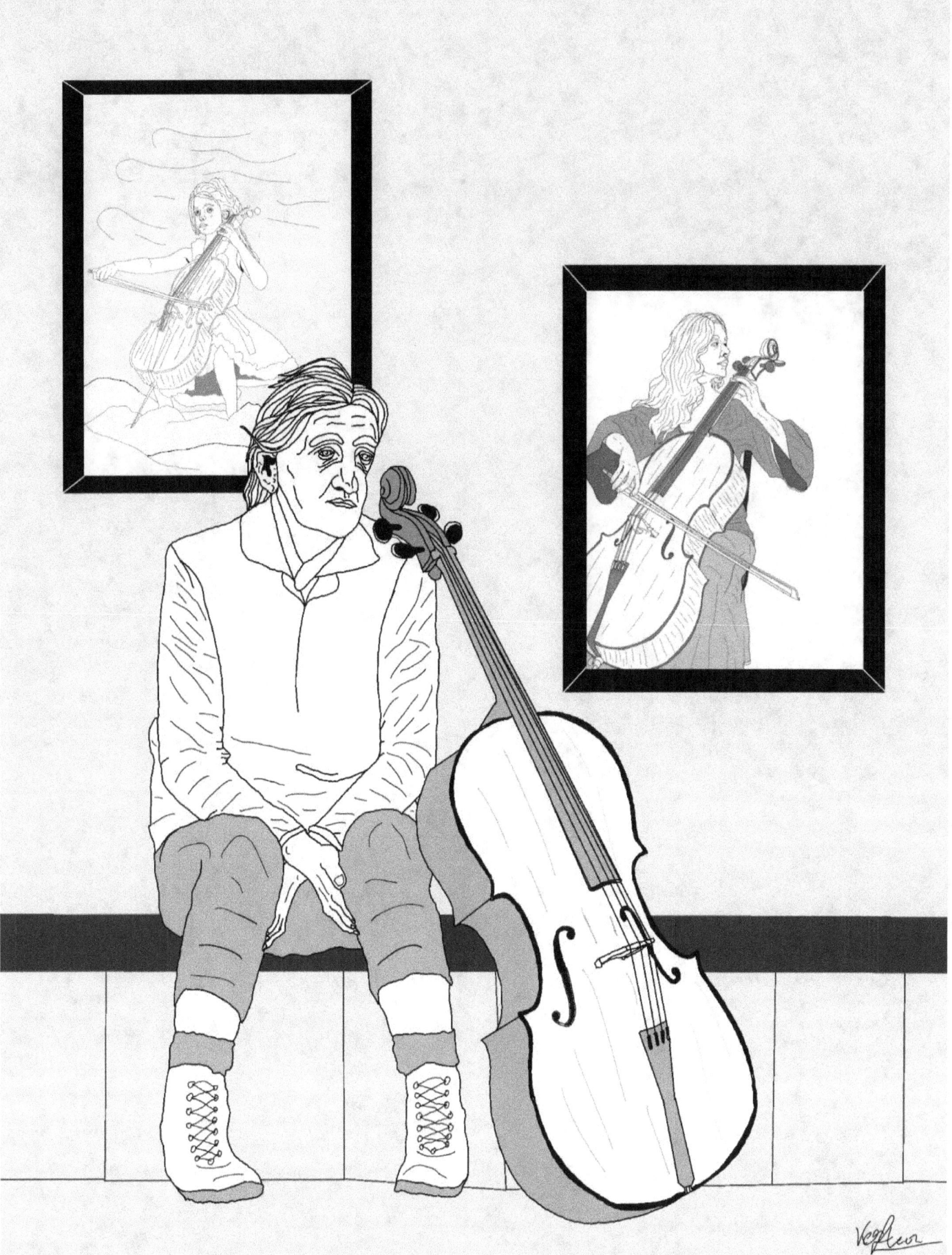

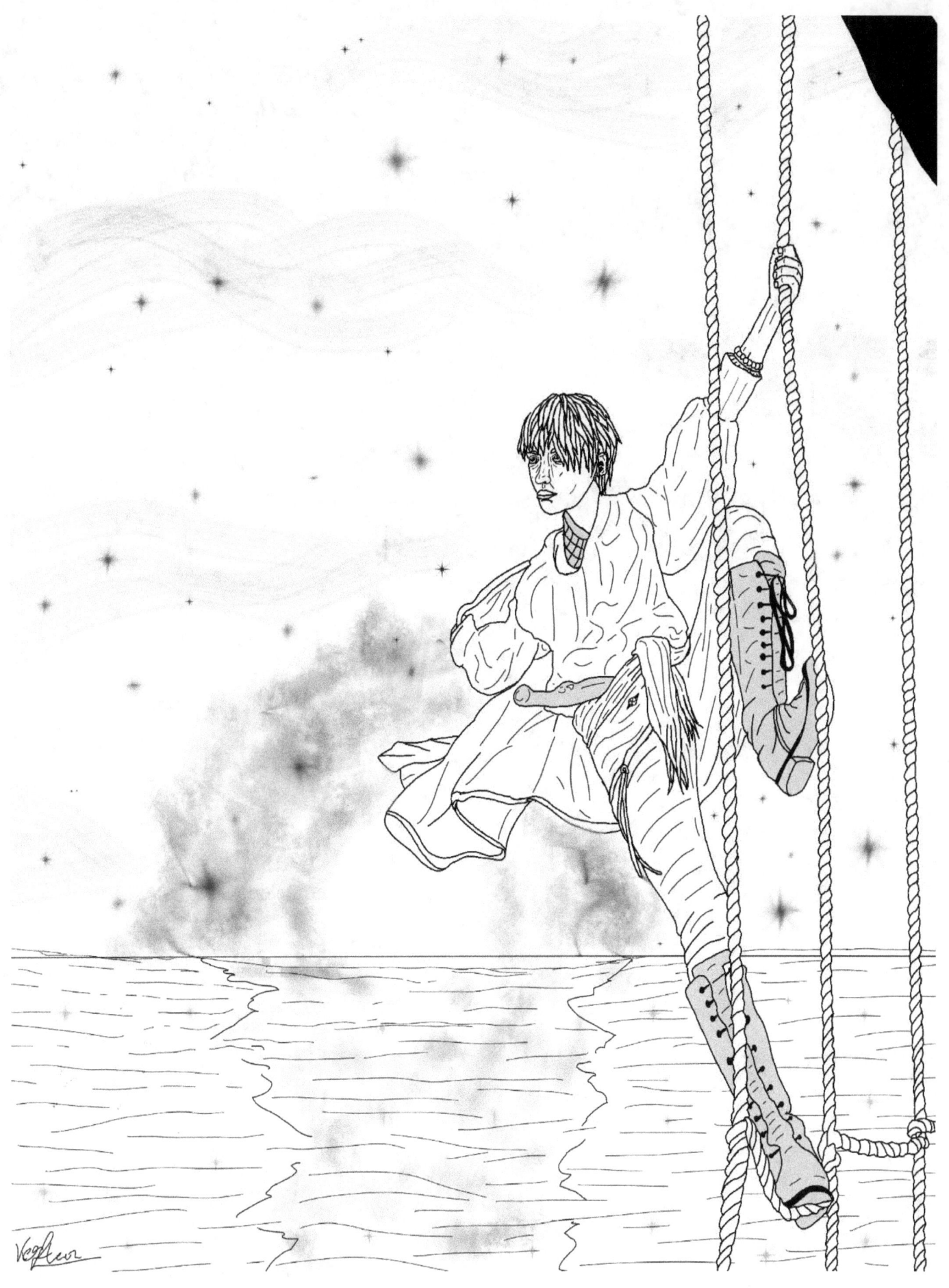

Kerwin is a self-taught French/American artist currently living in France. He has been dabbling in Digital Art for quite sometimes and has created an extensive collection of portraits. Each sketch is the result of an encounter with someone, be it in real life or on the net. He then puts his own spin on the subject and voilà….

You can follow him on Instagram or Etsy at Kerwessentials